Wilfrid Meynell, Henry Edward Manning

The Cardinal Archbishop of Westminster

Wilfrid Meynell, Henry Edward Manning

The Cardinal Archbishop of Westminster

ISBN/EAN: 9783743369146

Manufactured in Europe, USA, Canada, Australia, Japa

Cover: Foto ©Lupo / pixelio.de

Manufactured and distributed by brebook publishing software (www.brebook.com)

Wilfrid Meynell, Henry Edward Manning

The Cardinal Archbishop of Westminster

THE CARDINAL ARCHBISHOP

OF WESTMINSTER

WITH NOTES

BY

JOHN OLDCASTLE

"*But, to those men that loved him, sweet as summer.*"

BURNS AND OATES

LONDON	NEW YORK
GRANVILLE MANSIONS	CATHOLIC PUBLICATION SOCIETY CO.
ORCHARD STREET, W.	BARCLAY STREET.

The following Record, printed first in a Periodical, of which large editions have been exhausted, is now republished to meet a demand made for it in a more permanent form.

J. O.

Dedication.

TO

FATHER ANTONINUS WILLIAMS

PROVINCIAL OF THE ENGLISH DOMINICANS:

IN TOKEN

OF LOVE ETERNAL.

MAY DAY, 1886.

CONTENTS.

	PAGE
THE EVENT OF PASSION SUNDAY, 1851	5
PORTRAITS: FROM 1812 TO 1886	13
THE LETTERS OF THIRTY-FIVE YEARS	20
LANDMARKS OF A LIFETIME	88

THE CARDINAL ARCHBISHOP
OF
WESTMINSTER.

The Event of Passion Sunday, 1851.

THE greatest events of men's lives are told in the fewest words. It is rather with the minor things—into which just enough feeling enters to make them vital, but not enough to make them absolutely intimate—that the best and most abundant autobiographies are concerned. That this reticence is due less to the common human instinct of hiding treasure than to the limitations of language and to the restrictions imposed by the rules of art, is probable. For instance, we want to show, and not to hide, Religion; and it is therefore owing solely to the difficulty of subordinating great things to "treatment" by literary methods, that the mass of the Religious Poetry of the world—in which we might hope to find our largest literary riches—is in the main poor in literary quality, and is only in the exceptions, which all know, intimate, magical and penetrating.

Even in human love, the poet tells us that "the wise say least;" and this, not by any self-imposed restraint, but by the inexorable limitations of speech. It is only in novels that men and women are voluble at any real crisis of life. They are silent at the graveside; silent in the moment of supreme danger. The tenderest passages of love remain unspoken; for what man, when he proposed, " pleaded with an eloquence excelling that of all his Parliamentary speeches"—except only a hero of Lord Beaconsfield's ? Even great authors are unequal to the literary "treatment" of Love in its completion. A lost love, or a discarded love—they will tell of these; of love so long as it is doubtful; but love crowned by happy marriage brings the volume to a close.

Musicians tell us that their sounds possess a power of expression beyond that of speech. In music, they say, the history, not of the heart merely, but even of a soul, can be expressed. Yet that expression is itself a veil. If words cannot go quite so far, they are at least distinct and interpretable to their last limit; while music, if it goes further, is the earlier lost. Thus it comes to pass that we are ever dumb where alone we would be eloquent. Between spirit and spirit there can be no adequately intelligible medium of communication until the soul has burst from her prison. We must suffer "the silence of Christian transfigurations," and other silences as perplexing, a little yet. The mysteries of religion, after eighteen hundred years, remain mysteries still; and the reticence of Holy Scripture is the standing and Divine rebuke of those human pens which aspire to fantastically supply dear and dreamed-of incidents in the Life of Our Lord for which even Inspiration could not find the fitting phrase: which the Mother of the Eternal Word spoke not of, but only pondered in her heart.

It is with thoughts like these that we approach the event of Passion Sunday in the year of grace, 1851. Of what dies and of what is born within the convert when he makes, amid matter-of-fact surroundings, the great renunciation and the great acquisition of his life, no record can be made. Every man is conscious that there are places of decay and of fructification within him which he cannot define even to his own soul: they are lost upon his spiritual map, as the grave of Moses and Eden's garden are lost in the world. It is with no light or confident hand, therefore, that we place at the head of our chapter a title which implies so much of which we can tell so little. That little is perhaps best introduced by the words of a chronicler who wrote a few days after Archdeacon Manning's reception into the Church :

Mr. Manning has really attempted to work the Establishment upon Catholic principles in a high and important official position. But even he, with all his great position and his important connections, his prudence, his eloquence, his remarkable aptitude for and acquaintance with affairs, his forbearance, his patience and his holiness, has at last felt he could do nothing; that the Church of England is Protestant, and Protestant it will remain ; that it is not the Church of Augustine and Anselm, but of Cranmer and Burnet; that if men wish to be Catholics they must have recourse to the Chair of Peter, to the Roman Unity. But while we thus congratulate our readers on this important accession of one of the leading minds of the Anglican Establishment, we shall hardly have done our duty as journalists or as Catholics if we do not say something on the great, the heroic sacrifice this man has made for the sake of Catholic truth. He has given up all that is most dear to that lofty ambition which forms the peculiar temptation of minds of the noblest mould. A position exactly suited to his talents, of widely extended influence, and a splendid future ; the favour of men, and the almost certainty (had he preferred it to his conscience) of ultimately carrying out his views as Bishop; the devoted adherence of troops of friends; an abode as fair as any of those we see scattered over England and occupied by her ministers, fortunate in this world's goods; an abode amid calm streams and green woody hills, with that ancient village church, in its present state almost the creation of his genius and cultivated taste; all this, and far more, Mr. Manning has given up with a great heart, generous and liberal to Almighty God, Who has been so liberal of graces to him, counting all as nothing so he may fight in the Holy Catholic Church now that he has seen her star in the distance. He has not, like others, pointed the way to Bethlehem, and then refused to go thither himself.

So wrote Mr. Lucas in the *Tablet*, in April 1851. With the facts fresh in all minds, he did not make formal record of the episode which more than any other had led up to the conversion of Archdeacon Manning. This was the decision by which Mr. Gorham, though he denied baptismal regeneration, was permitted to remain a minister of the Anglican Communion. In March 1850 Archdeacon Manning and his brother-in-law, the late Henry Wilberforce, conferring with Mr. Gladstone and other friends, drew up resolutions condemnatory of that decision. The document stated that "to admit the lawfulness of holding an exposition of an Article of the Creed contradictory of the essential meaning of that Article, is in truth and in fact to abandon that Article;" and "inasmuch as the faith is one, and rests upon one principle of authority, the conscious, deliberate, and wilful abandonment of an Article destroys the divine foundation upon which alone the entire faith is propounded;" and that "any portion of the Church which does so abandon an Article forfeits not only the Catholic doctrine in that Article, but also the office and authority to witness and teach as a member of the Universal Church."

There are thirteen names attached to that manifesto, and they are these: H. E. Manning, R. I. Wilberforce, Thomas Thorp, W. H. Mill, E. B. Pusey, John Keble, W. Dodsworth, W. J. E. Bennett, Henry Wilberforce, J. C. Talbot, Richard Cavendish, Edward Badeley and James R. Hope (afterwards Hope-Scott). But vainly was the protest made. The civil power was supreme, and who should gainsay it? Six of the signatories attested their sincerity by submitting to the Catholic Church. But, like the bulk of the Anglican clergy who shared the convictions the manifesto expressed, the majority of the signatories themselves refused to carry their principles into effect. One of these is still alive, vehement as ever—witness his recent fiery onslaught upon Mr. Gladstone, with whom he then acted sympathetically. And, speaking of Archdeacon Denison, I allow myself to quote—since it is cognate to my theme— one of the finest passages in the library of Tractarianism —which was a literary movement only less than it was a religious one. In his story of "A Life's Decision" Mr. Allies writes :

I was present at a large meeting in a public resort at Westminster, on February 7, 1850, just before the issue of the Gorham judgment. The air was charged with the coming report, and one gallant speaker especially distinguished himself. If, he said, they ventured to touch the doctrine of baptismal regeneration, they would see what would happen. He dared them to the trial. The speaker was applauded to the echo. A movement swept over the assembly of which he was the mouthpiece.

In a few days the judgment came out, which was simply that ministers of the Anglican religion might preach or deny baptismal regeneration, as they listed. Nobody should touch them for teaching or for contradicting it. What did the speaker do? He issued a protest, which was moonshine; for nothing followed on his part. Yes, I forgot, something did follow; he accepted an archdeaconry from a partially sympathetic bishop. And once upon a time he stood forward as a champion for the doctrine of the Real Presence, maintaining that it was a doctrine of the Anglican Church. His challenge was taken up. But when the trial was coming on, his courage failed. It appeared that his act of challenge was more than two years old, and the law provided him with a retreat. This was the cloud which received the warrior. Forthwith this dainty Paris

ἂψ ἑτάρων εἰς ἔθνος ἐχάζετο, κῆρ ἀλεείνων.

Since then he has been toying with the fair destroyer, "the hell of ships, of men, of cities," the Helen, whose charms grow not old. From his well-provisioned fortress, as Bishop's Eye, he surveys the adverse towers of his cathedral city, where an unsympathetic bishop has succeeded; marks how the flood of unbelief advances, and mourns that he has seen during every year of a long life the principles which he holds to be true decline and be frustrated.

I do not mention him as in any point of view less consistent than any other member of that large company addressed by Father Newman in 1850, who held the leading principles of the "Tracts of the Times;" but I take him as a lively symbol of what all have done. And I ask, is this, indeed, a Life Worth Living? Yet it is the life of many thousands who have lived and died between 1850 and 1880, and of many thousands more who are still detained in Helen's bower.

O Church of the living God, Pillar and Ground of the Truth, fair as the moon, bright as the sun, terrible as an army in battle array, O Mother of Saints and Doctors, Martyrs and Virgins, clothe thyself in the robe and aspect, as thou hast the strength, of Him Whose Body thou art, the Love for our sake incarnate: shine forth upon thy lost children, and draw them to the double fountain of thy bosom, the well-spring of Truth and Grace!

That final passage is one to be incorporated in the living Literature of the Church—a passage to place beside the words of Basil and of Augustine and of Chrysostom— the golden-mouthed.

The ex-Archdeacon of Chichester has never given to the world a full history of the growth of his religious opinions. He has left them to be implied by his toils rather than be stated by tongue or pen. We are nevertheless able to give in his own words some outline of the experiences which ended at Farm Street just thirty-five years ago—so happily for England and for him :

> The sacredness and sovereignty of divine faith makes it a duty to use words as the sincere medium of thoughts, and to use the fewest and the simplest that will convey our meaning. In such words I endeavoured for many years to say all that I knew of Truth to those who then would listen to me. I have had no other motive than a perpetual and ardent desire to give to others the truth as God has given it to me. I am fully conscious of the great imperfection of the books which I wrote while as yet I knew the revelation of the day of Pentecost only in a broken and fragmentary way. As I saw the truth, so I spoke it; not without cost to myself. But I had no choice. I could not but declare that which was evidently to me "the truth as it is in Jesus." The works I then published, even without the private records I have by me, are enough to mark the progressive, but slow, and never receding advance of my convictions, from the first conception of a visible Church, its succession and witness for Christ, to the full perception and manifestation of its divine organization of Head and members, of its supernatural prerogatives of indefectible life, indissoluble unity, infallible discernment, and enunciation of the Faith. Of those books I will say nothing, but that even in their great imperfections they have an unity, that is of progress, and a directness of movement, always affirming positively and definitely such truths of the perfect revelation of God as successively arose upon me. I was as one *manu tentans, meridie cæcutiens*, but a divine Guide, as yet unknown to me, always led me on. I can well remember how at the outset of my life as a pastor, as I then already believed, the necessity of a divine commission forced itself upon me : next, how the necessity of a divine certainty for the message I had to deliver became, if possible, more evident. A divine, that is, an infallible message, by a human messenger is still the truth of God ; but a human, or fallible message, by a messenger having a divine commission, would be the source of error, illusion, and all evil. I then perceived the principle of Christian tradition as an evidence of the Truth, and of the visible unity of the Church as the guarantee of that tradition. But it was many years before I perceived that such a Christian tradition was no more than human, and therefore fallible. I had reached the last point to which human history could guide me towards the Church of God. There

remained one point more, to know that the Church is not only a human witness in the order of history, but a divine witness in the order of supernatural facts. It was not my intention, when I began, to enter into these details. I have never done so in public till now, and I hardly know whether to cancel what I have written, or to proceed in what I have to say. I have never thought it necessary to publish the reasons of my submission to the Church of God. I felt that those who knew me knew my reasons, for they had followed my words and acts: and that they who did not know me would not care to know. I felt, too, that the best expositor of a man's conduct is his life; and that in a few years, and in the way of duty, I should naturally and unconsciously make clear and intelligible to all who care to know, the motives of faith which governed me in that time of public and private trial.

And yet when all is written, how little is written. When we have heard all that is said, how much remains that can never be said. And so it is in other things as well as in the history of great spiritual changes. A kindred sense of dumbness comes over the chronicler who would make, on behalf of English-speaking Catholics, a record of the loyalty and the love and the long gratitude they owe their spiritual Father, and daily pay in many a thought and many a prayer. Then, when words come from a pen that has no magic to vivify them, at least let those words be few. And there is this consolation—that they are Pharisees among scribes, as well as among suppliants, who think they shall be heard for their much speaking.

Portraits: From 1812 to 1886.

1812.

THE charming portrait which bears the date of 1812 shows the future Cardinal Archbishop as a little boy listening to a shell : and the "message from the sea" it told him could not be a more astonishing revelation than that of his own destiny. The original miniature, from which our reproduction is made, was one of a group of similar portraits of his Eminence's brothers and sisters. They hung together on the wall of the library of his father's house at Totteridge, until one night when they were stolen. Lost sight of for some years, they were at last discovered by chance in a second-hand shop in London, and happily reclaimed. The original of this particular portrait is now in the possession of his Eminence's sister-in-law, Mrs. Charles Manning.

1844.

The portrait of the Archdeacon of Chichester was painted by Mr. Richmond, and issued by Mr. Hogarth as an engraving, of which impressions can still be obtained from Messrs. Burns & Oates. It shows the future Cardinal at a time when he was regarded as the great champion of the liberties of the English Establishment. Bishop Philpotts, of Exeter, was wont to say then that there were three men to whom the country had mainly to look in the coming years—Manning in the Church, Gladstone in the State, and Hope in the Law. When the Archdeacon and Hope-Scott left the Church of England, Gladstone, who stayed behind, said he felt as if he had lost his two eyes. Another Anglican Bishop, Hamilton of Salisbury,

1812.

writing many years later to Mr. Hope-Scott, said: "Few trials of my life have I felt with such keenness as my separation from two such friends, from whom I have learnt so much, and whom I have loved and love so dearly, as Manning and yourself." Nor was it only High Churchmen who were drawn to the Archdeacon. Julius Hare, a " Broad " neighbouring dignitary, equally hailed him as counsellor and friend. "Manning," he said, "is a truly wise and holy man—zealous, devoted, self-sacrificing, and gentle." Those personal characteristics, at any rate, have not changed. In outward aspect, time and circumstance have made their mark; but among all the portraits of seventy-five years the likeness is easily traceable—even between the child of three or four and the venerable Churchman of to-day, with the connecting link of the portrait of the Archdeacon. In that portrait will be perceived the look of perplexity which, as a great writer noted, passed away when the Archdeacon came out from the City of Confusion.

1875.

The portrait dated 1875 was taken immediately after the Archbishop had been created a Cardinal, and it shows him in the dress in which he appears, on ordinary occasions, "In the pulpit."

1885 and 1886.

Of the later portraits, that which is dated 1885 (from a photograph by Mayall) shows his Eminence as he appears "At home," when he wears in the cold weather a coat over his cassock; while the frontispiece (from a photograph by Bassano) portrays his Eminence as he appears "At the Royal Commission," and on similar occasions.

1844.

PEN AND INK PORTRAIT BY LORD BEACONSFIELD.

Speaking, as we did just now, of the altered mien of the Manning of old days, and that of the Roman Prelate of later times, we recall a passage in Mr. Mozley's fascinating *Reminiscences*, in which he says:—"I had known him, as a friend of the Wilberforces, from his first coming to Oxford, and had frequently heard him at the Union. It is not easy for me to identify the Manning of my early recollections with the Father of the Vatican Council whom I heard preach at the Church of Isidore on St. Patrick's Day. He must have grown taller and his head larger since he was a very nice-looking, rather boyish freshman." Is it a curious coincidence merely, or another evidence of the real pains which Lord Beaconsfield sometimes took over the details of his delineations, that such an impression as that of Mr. Mozley—"he must have grown taller"—finds a place also in the sketch of the Archbishop of Tyre in *Endymion?* With that pen-portrait—which is a better one throughout than its forerunner in *Lothair*, drawn when the Statesman was less intimate with the Churchman than he became in his last years—we supplement and complete the counterfeit presentments of his Eminence here made:—

They were speaking of Nigel Penruddock, whose movements had been a matter of much mystery during the last two years. Rumours of his having been received into the Roman Church had been rife; sometimes flatly, and in time faintly contradicted. Now the fact seemed admitted, and it would appear that he was about to return to England, not only as a Roman Catholic, but as a distinguished priest of the Church; and, it was said, even the representative of the Papacy. Nigel was changed. Instead of that anxious and moody look which formerly marred the refined beauty of his countenance, his glance was calm and yet radiant. He was thinner, it might almost be said emaciated, which seemed to add height to his tall figure. . . . . All he spoke of was the magnitude of his task, the immense but inspiring labours which awaited him, and his deep sense of his responsibility. Nothing but the Divine principle of the Church could sustain him. Instead of avoiding society, as was his wont in old days, the Archbishop sought it. And there was nothing exclusive in his social habits; all classes and all creeds and all conditions of men were alike interesting to him; they were part of the community, with all whose pursuits, and passions, and interests, and occupations he seemed to sympathise; but respecting which he had

1875.

only one object—to bring them back once more to that imperial fold from which, in an hour of darkness and distraction, they had miserably wandered. The conversion of England was deeply engraven on the heart of Penruddock; it was his constant purpose and his daily and nightly prayer. So the Archbishop was seen everywhere, even at fashionable assemblies. He was a frequent guest at banquets, which he never tasted, for he was a smiling ascetic; and though he seemed to be preaching or celebrating Mass in every part of the metropolis, organising schools, establishing convents, and building cathedrals, he could find time to move resolutions at middle-class meetings, attend learned associations, and even send a paper to the Royal Society.

The Letters of Thirty-five Years.

"I TRUST TO BE LED TO THE TRUTH."

To T. W. ALLIES, M.A.

Lavington, *June* 19, 1850.

MY DEAR ALLIES,

Your letter* came at a time when I was obliged to delay writing, and since then until to-day I have been absent, travelling, and so overdone with writing that I could not answer it before.

The question you put appears to be, whether on the points you mention I know any considerations which might alter your conclusion.

This would require, as we said in London, a verifying of the matter of your premises, and a further statement of them than I have. But certainly your book upon the question of Schism is, to my mind, ample ground for doubting any contrary conclusion without more evidence than I have yet seen.

But I feel myself so much to need the same re-examination myself, that I hope to enter upon it with a single intention to

---

* Mr. Allies had written from Launton Rectory to Archdeacon Manning a letter in which he said: "I find at least five different points, more or less involving each other and widely branching, but each *capital*, on which I am unable to acquit the Church of England. These are the questions: (1) Of Unity; and, involved in it, (2) Of Infallibility; (3) Of Heresy; (4) Of Schism; (5) Of Jurisdiction (that is, the substitution of Royal for Papal supremacy—in the case of Parker, &c.). I consider that to be wrong in *any one* of these points cuts off a province of the Church from all the privileges of the one mystical body. What, then, and how great is the cumulative force of all five?" (See "A Life's Decision" for the whole narrative of Mr. Allies' conversion.)

obey the truth and will of God with all my heart. If I could offer to you anything you have not weighed, I would, gladly; but you have, I know, far outgone me in real study. My life, as you know, has been active to excess, and you would hardly believe how little has been my time for reading. This makes me thoroughly mistrust myself; and the heavier the crisis and its consequences, the more I turn to others to review and test my conclusions or opinions. All that I can say is that my time has been given to "serving my neighbour"—how poorly I well know.

This is a worthless letter to send you; but I have no better. I trust to be led to the truth in these points, on which I feel to need rather than to be able to give such help as you require.

May God be with you, my dear Allies, that all you do may be according to His will, and bring you to peace at the last.

Give me your prayers always, as I am sure you will, for old and kind memory's sake.

Believe me ever yours affectionately,

H. E. MANNING.

"LET ME HAVE YOUR PRAYERS."

To T. W. ALLIES, M.A.

Kippington, Sevenoaks, *September* 20, 1850.

MY DEAR ALLIES,

Though I have not written, I have not forgotten you day by day. We have been too closely united, and I have known too much of your past trials, for me to be unmoved by anything so deeply affecting you.* May God bless and keep you to the end!

---

* Mr. Allies had been received into the Catholic Church twelve days before by Father Newman at St. Wilfrid's, Maryvale, near Birmingham.

Many thanks for the enclosed letters, which are very thoughtful and interesting, and also for your book ("The See of St. Peter.") I have read it once, and shall read it again closely, and with the examination you would desire. It is very able, and demands a full treatment by any one who will answer it. Let me have your prayers, that I may know and do the will of God in all things.

Believe me always affectionately yours,

H. E. MANNING.

"IT SHALL NOT BE DONE IN LIGHTNESS."

To J. R. HOPE-SCOTT, Q.C.

Lavington, *Nov.* 23, 1850.

MY DEAR HOPE,

Your last letter was a help to me, for I began to feel as if every man had gone to his own house, and left the matter. . . . .

Since then, events have driven me to a decision. This Anti-Popery cry has seized my brethren, and they asked me to be convened.* I must either resign at once, or convene them

---

* The Re-establishment of the Catholic Hierarchy had thrown the country into an anti-Popery fever, of which the futile Ecclesiastical Titles Bill was the Parliamentary expression. Cardinal Newman thus described what was passing at the time :—" Heresy, and scepticism, and infidelity, and fanaticism, may challenge the Establishment; but fling upon the gale the faintest whisper of Catholicism, and it recognizes by instinct the presence of its connatural foe. Forthwith, as during the last year, the atmosphere is tremulous with agitation, and discharges its vibrations far and wide. A movement is in birth which has no natural crisis or resolution. Spontaneously the bells of the steeples begin to sound. Not by an act of volition, but by a sort of mechanical impulse, bishop and dean, archdeacon and canon, rector and curate, one after another, each on his high tower, off they set, swinging and booming, tolling and chiming, with nervous intenseness, and thickening emotion, and deepening volume, the old ding-dong which has scared town and country this weary time; tolling and chiming away, jingling and

ministerially and express my dissent, the reasons of which would involve my resignation. I went to the Bishop, and said this, and tendered my resignation. He was very kind, and wished me to take time; but I have written and made it final.

I should be glad if we might keep together; and whatever must be done, do it with a calm and deliberateness which shall give testimony that it shall not be done in lightness.

Ever affectionately yours,
H. E. M.

"EITHER ROME, OR LICENSE OF THOUGHT AND WILL."

To J. R. HOPE-SCOTT, Q.C.

[*Private.*]

44 Cadogan Place, *December* 11, 1850.

MY DEAR HOPE,

I feel, with you, that the argument is complete. For a long time I nevertheless felt a fear lest I should be doing an act morally wrong.

This fear has passed away, because the Church of England has revealed itself in a way to make me fear more on the other side. It remains, therefore, as an act of the will. But this, I suppose, it must be. And in making it I am helped by the clamouring and ringing the changes on their poor half-dozen notes, all about 'the Popish aggression,' 'insolent and insidious,' 'insidious and insolent,' 'insolent and atrocious,' 'atrocious and insolent,' 'atrocious, insolent, and ungrateful,' 'ungrateful, insolent, and atrocious,' 'foul and offensive,' 'pestilent and horrid,' 'subtle and unholy,' 'audacious and revolting,' 'contemptible and shameless,' 'malignant,' 'frightful,' 'mad,' 'meretricious'—bobs (I think the ringers call them), bobs, and bobs-royal, and triple-bob-majors, and grandsires—to the extent of their compass and the full ring of their metal, in honour of Queen Bess, and to the confusion of the Holy Father and the Princes of the Church." In such a fussy fight, the innate dignity of the Archdeacon of Chichester, apart from doctrinal questionings, must by itself have incapacitated him for the post of fugleman.

fact, that to remain under our changed or revealed circumstances would also be an act of the will, and that not in conformity with, but in opposition to, intellectual real conviction ; and the intellect is God's gift, and our instrument in attaining knowledge of His will. .... It would be to me a very great happiness if we could act together, and our names go together in the first publication of the fact. .... The subject which has brought me to my present convictions is the perpetual office of the Church, under Divine guidance, in expounding the truth and deciding controversies. And the book which forced this on me, Melchior Canus' "Loci Theologici." It is a long book, but so orderly that you may get the whole outline with ease. Möhler's " Symbolik," you know.

But, after all, Holy Scripture comes to me in a new light, as Ephes. iv. 4–17, which seems to preclude the notion of a divisible unity ; which is, in fact, Arianism in the matter of the Church.

I entirely feel what you say of the alternative. It is either Rome, or license of thought and will. . . .

Believe me always affectionately yours,

H. E. MANNING.

"THIS MORNING, BY GOD'S MERCY."

To T. W. ALLIES, M.A.

14 Queen Street, Mayfair,
Passion Sunday, 1851.

MY DEAR ALLIES,

Others, I fear, will have been before me in telling you of my intention, but I may be the first to tell you that this morning, by God's mercy, I entered the One True Fold.

I have felt your consideration towards my sister in not coming to see me; but now, and here, I shall be delighted to see you again.

Pray for me that I may be kept in the grace of God.

Ever yours affectionately,

H. E. MANNING.

"NO DESIRE UNFULFILLED."

To J. R. HOPE-SCOTT, Q.C.

14 Queen Street, *April* 7, 1851.

MY DEAR HOPE,

Will you accept this copy of the book you saw in my room yesterday [the "Paradisus Animæ"], in memory of Passion Sunday and its gift of grace to us? It is the most perfect book of devotion I know. Let me ask one thing. I read it through, one page at least a day, between January 26 and August 22, 1846, marking where I left off with the dates. It seemed to give me a new science, with order and harmony and details, as of devotion issuing from and returning into dogma. Could you burden yourself with the same resolution? If so, do it for my sake, and remember me when you do it.

I feel as if I had no desire unfulfilled, but to persevere in what God has given me for His Son's sake.

Believe me, my dear Hope,

Always aff'ly yours,

H. E. M.

"THE ONLY HUMAN HELP."

To J. R. HOPE-SCOTT, Q.C.

14 Queen Street, *October* 21, 1851.

. . . I am once more in my old quarters. They bring back strange remembrances. What revolutions have passed since we started from this room that Saturday morning! And how blessed an end! as the soul said to Dante. *E da martirio venni a questa pace.* . . . You do not need that I should say how sensibly I remember all your sympathy, which was the only human help in the time when we two went together through the trial, which to be known must be endured.

H. E. MANNING.

"NO MISTAKE."

To J. R. HOPE-SCOTT, Q.C.

Rome, March 17, 1852.

. . . How this time reminds me of last year! On Passion Sunday I shall be in Retreat. *Stantes erant pedes nostri;* * and we made no mistake in our long reckoning, though we feared it up to the last opening of Fr. B.'s † door.

H. E. M.

PLANNING THE BAYSWATER COMMUNITY.

To J. R. HOPE-SCOTT, Q.C.

78 South Audley Street, January 28, 1856.

. . . Do you remember a conversation, the summer of 1854, one Sunday evening, at 22 Charles Street, on the good which might be done by four or five men living together and preaching statedly at different places on courses of solid subjects?

---

* These words were written in a copy of the "Speculum Vitæ Sacerdotalis" given by J. R. Hope to H. E. Manning, in April 1851. [Note by his Eminence].

† Father Brownbill, S.J., who had received Archdeacon Manning and Mr. Hope-Scott at the Church of the Jesuit Fathers in Farm Street on Passion Sunday, 1851.

The thought has long been in my mind, both before and since our conversation, and it has been coming to a point under an increased sense of the need.

H. E. M.

A DEDICATION.

To the late ROBERT MONTEITH, *of Carstairs.**

St. Mary of the Angels, Bayswater,
Christmas 1859.

DEAR MR. MONTEITH,

No one can feel more than I do how little worthy the following sermon is as a statement of the great truths contained in it; and but for the wish of others, I should rather have let it pass with the day which called for it.

But if it shall help to keep in your mind the happiness of a day in which you made your beautiful and noble offering to the Church of God in Scotland, or to show to so much as one of the many who, though "not of us," were with us that day, that the true Headship and Sovereignty of Jesus Christ over His Kingdom is to be found alone in the One Church which is

---

* The late Mr. Monteith belonged to one of the great banking families of Glasgow. In early life he had meditated entering Parliament, but he was deterred from doing so by the fact that the serious errors of a Cabinet Minister in relation to Foreign policy passed unreproved under our system of party government. To the end of his life he was deeply interested in Foreign affairs, and his last act was to draw up his *Discourse on the Shedding of Blood*, the humane principles of which he had warmly advocated in Rome, in conjunction with his friend the late Mr. David Urquhart, at the time of the Vatican Council. After his conversion to the Catholic Church, Mr. Monteith was distinguished by his charities, one of which is commemorated by this dedication of the sermon preached by the Cardinal at the opening of the Church of the Immaculate Conception at Lanark. It was in the grounds at Carstairs that the Rev. and Hon. George Spencer—dear to Catholics as Father Ignatius—met with the sudden and unattended death which completed the programme of austerity he had planned and prayed for as applicable to his holy life.

Catholic and Roman, I shall not regret letting it, with all its insufficiency, go abroad.

Believe me always
Very sincerely yours,
H. E. MANNING.

"LOVE FOR THE RELIGIOUS ORDERS."

To the VERY REV. NORBERT SWEENY, O.S.B.

St. Mary of the Angels, Bayswater,
Feast of the Guardian Angels, 1860.

DEAR FATHER PRIOR,

When you desired me to take a part in your great festival, I answered that I would with much willingness do your bidding, as a token of my love and veneration for the Religious Orders of the Church, and especially in England; and in printing this sermon* at your request, I do so as offering to you and to them a *tessera charitatis*, and that we may obtain in return a share in your charity and your prayers.

Believe me always
Your affectionate servant in Jesus Christ,
HENRY EDWARD MANNING.

THE OBLATES OF ST. CHARLES IN LONDON.

To NICHOLAS, FIRST CARDINAL-ARCHBISHOP OF WESTMINSTER.

St. Mary of the Angels, Bayswater,
November 14, 1860.

MY LORD CARDINAL,

In dedicating this sermon † to your Eminence, I do not

---

* "Unity in Diversity the Perfection of the Church," preached at the consecration of the Priory and Pro-Cathedral of St. Michael's, Hereford, 1860.

† "The Good Shepherd," preached in the Church of St. Mary of the Angels, Bayswater, on the Feast of St. Charles, 1860.

seek to give it either worth or importance, which even your name could not do. But to whom can I better inscribe it than to you, the father and founder of the Oblates of St. Charles in the Diocese of Westminster? It was your command alone that constrained me to attempt a work which I know to have been for more than twenty years in your intention. Your name obtained for it, in the outset, a rescript of the Holy See, imparting the apostolical benediction; your counsel has directed it; and your authority guided all its course.

The Feast of St. Charles has never passed without your presence, except last year, when from your bed of sickness you wrote to us your words of encouragement and support. And this year, after twelve months, as I too well know, of perilous and protracted suffering, you came again among us to share and to complete the joy of our festival.

As a record of our gratitude for all these tokens of your affection, I pray you to accept from me, in the name of all, this imperfect expression of our filial attachment.

I have the honour to be, my Lord Cardinal,

Your Eminence's obedient servant,

H. E. MANNING.

"VERY DEAR, AS LIFE IS DRAWING TO ITS CLOSE."

(*To the Editor of* THE PALL MALL GAZETTE.)

York Place, Portman Square,

Nov. 3, 1866.

SIR,

I have read "Bocardo's" letter about the debate on Shelley's merits at Oxford, and can confirm your correspondent's recollection in most points by my own. Nevertheless, I do not believe that I was guilty of the rashness of throwing the javelin over the Cam. It was, I think, a passage of arms got up by the Eton men of the two Unions. My share—if any—was only as a member of the august committee of the green baize table. I can, however, well remember the irruption of the three Cambridge orators.

We Oxford men were precise, orderly, and morbidly afraid of excess in word or manner. The Cambridge oratory came in like a flood into a mill-pond. Both Monckton Milnes and Henry Hallam took us aback by the boldness and freedom of their manner. But I remember the effect of Sunderland's declamation and action to this day. It had never been seen or heard before among us; we cowered like birds and ran like sheep. I was reminding, the other day, the Secretary of the India Board of the damage he did me. He was my private tutor, and was terrifically sitting right opposite to me. I had just rounded a period when I saw him make, as I believed in my agony, a sign of contempt, which all but brought me down. I acknowledge that we were utterly routed. Lord Houghton's beautiful reviving of those old days has in it something fragrant and sweet, and brings back old faces and old friendships, very dear as life is drawing to its close.

Your faithful servant,
HENRY E. MANNING.

"PRAYERS FOR ORIENTALS."

To the Rev. F. TONDINI, of the Congregation of the Fathers Barnabites.

8 York Place, Portman Square,
London, W., *November* 7, 1866.

REV. AND DEAR FATHER,

I have the greatest pleasure in giving my approbation to the Association of Prayers for the Conversion of Oriental

Schismatics, and especially of the Russians and Greeks, to the Catholic Faith and Unity, and in granting forty days' indulgence to all who shall co-operate with you in spreading the Association in the diocese of Westminster by reciting the prayer to our Immaculate Mother with that intention.

Be so good as to enrol my name in the Association. At this time, when the thought and desire of union is so active in the minds of men, I rejoice to see so truly and purely Catholic an Association extending in the midst of us. I am glad also to see it introduced among us by a spiritual son of the B. Alexander Sauli, the friend of S. Charles; this gives us the true re-union of Christendom on the basis of Trent, in submission to the Sovereign Pontiff, and under the intercession of the most Blessed and Immaculate Mother of God.

I heartily pray that God may bless you and your work,

And remain, Rev. and dear Father,

Your affectionate servant in Christ,

HENRY EDWARD,

Archbishop of Westminster.

"A TEST OF LOVE."

To Father HERBERT VAUGHAN.*

November 23, 1871.

MY DEAR FATHER VAUGHAN,

While I am sending this book to press, you are on the Atlantic, conducting the first band of Missionary Fathers from St. Joseph's College to their work among the Negroes.

---

* Now Bishop of Salford. The sermons thus inscribed to his Lordship are—"Our Duty to the Heathen," "Missions to the Heathen: a Test of Love," and "The Negro Mission;" two of which were preached at the great Missionary College of St. Joseph at Mill Hill. The whole are to be found in *Sermons on Ecclesiastical Subjects* (Burns and Oates).

I therefore cannot refrain from putting into this volume the three following sermons, not for any worth in them, but because they were preached at your request, and because they enable me to express what we owe to you for the founding of our first seminary for missions to the heathen. They will be, I hope, a permanent appeal to the charity and alms of the faithful in behalf of your great work; and perhaps some one who reads them may help to finish your church, or may found a burse for the education of a missionary.

May God prosper you, and bring you home in safety.

Believe me always

Yours very affectionately in Christ,

HENRY EDWARD,

Archbishop of Westminster.

CERTAIN VISIONS.

To the Editor of THE TIMES.

Archbishop's House, S.W., *Sept.* 8, 1873.

SIR,

When the letter of a correspondent of the *Times* * is embodied in the same type and in the same column with one of its leading communications, it may be assumed to be hardly less than editorial.

"Senex Anglicanus" asks of me a question. He has a full right to ask it, as I have a full right to decline to answer. But I have not the least inducement to withhold my reply: first because I can answer it at once; and next, because I thank him for giving me the opportunity of calling your attention to an error in the leading article of the *Times* of Wednesday last.

---

* A letter signed "Senex Anglicanus" had appeared in the *Times*, in which the writer charged the Archbishop with "shrinking from the avowal of his belief in the miraculous apparition of Paray."

"Senex Anglicanus" asks of me, why, in relating the vision upon which the devotion of the Sacred Heart is founded, I passed "in total silence" over the vision which in your leading article of Wednesday last you described as the foundation of the devotion, and as a "physical operation, grotesque and extravagant."

My reason was this: That the vision you quoted is not the vision upon which the devotion was founded.

Of this "Senex Anglicanus" may satisfy himself by referring to the Life of the Blessed Margaret Mary, by the Rev. George Tickell (Burns and Oates, 1869, p. 151). In the Life of the Blessed Margaret Mary about seventy visions are recorded. I had no reason to quote any but the one in which this devotion had its origin.

Allow me now, in turn, to put a question to "Senex Anglicanus." Why did you, knowing so little on this subject, venture to write the following words?—

"What is to be thought of a reticence which bears so strong a likeness to studied evasion? No doubt the Archbishop found himself in a very difficult and perplexing position. He had strong reasons for shrinking from the avowal of his belief in such a story. He had still stronger motives for avoiding the slightest intimation of a doubt which would have ruined his character at Rome, and have exposed him to the danger of being torn to pieces by Veuillot. If he has succeeded in extricating himself from the difficulty, it is by a kind of dexterity which might be admirable in a Cagliostro, but which is not exactly that which people expect in an Archbishop."

In your article, sir, of Wednesday last, you published a *spicilegium* of what you thought hard words, uttered by me, deserved, as I think, by those who may be guilty of the faults I then censured. The passages above quoted are a fair example of the conduct of those whom I was describing, as critics who are in too great haste to condemn, and, like men who are precipitate, stammer not only with their lips, but also with their pens and their intellect. The hypothetical form of the quotations I have given does not clear them from the worst-known kind of false witness—I mean insinuation of motives.

It is somewhat refreshing to me to be charged with reticence in any matter relating to what some people are pleased to call Popery ; and though I have sufficiently answered the question of "Senex Anglicanus," I will also answer his question as to what you have thought fit to describe as a "physical operation."

The vision you refer to is one, as I have said, in a multitude vouchsafed to the Blessed Margaret Mary. Those visions, as you are well aware, are not and cannot be matter of Divine faith ; for this reason, because they do not rest upon the revelation of God. Nevertheless, I fully believe them to be true.

First, because they rest upon evidence sufficient to command our belief as to the facts in the history of a person.

Secondly, because that evidence has passed under repeated and rigorous examination by competent authorities on the spot and in Rome.

Thirdly, because in the matter of those visions there is nothing that is not consistent with visions and Divine actions recorded in the Old and in the New Testament.

Your correspondent I assume to be a member of the Church of England, and he states himself to be of mature age. I may therefore further assume that he has not taken advantage of the principles of Biblical criticism sanctioned by the highest judicial authority in the realm some years ago. He does not, therefore, separate the subject-matter of Holy Scripture into inspired and uninspired, into Divine and human, into credible and incredible. He will not deny that visions, if true, are at all times acts of omnipotence, and that no human intelligence can prescribe limits to their effect. It will be well for him to read over again the twenty-first and twenty-second verses of the second chapter of Genesis, also the twenty-fifth verse of the thirty-second chapter of the same book, and the twenty-seventh verse of the twentieth chapter of St. John's Gospel.

It is neither wise nor safe in those who profess to believe in a Creator and a Redeemer, and that He is the Lord and Disposer of all things which He has made and redeemed, to use arguments which overturn both the old creation and the new.

I am not going to enter, in the columns of the *Times*, upon a discussion of things so sacred. You, sir, though on some occasions somewhat peremptory and despotic, are never irreverent. Your columns are never stained with the trivial mockery which I sometimes read with shame in our papers. When we have the ill fate to be in opposition I recognize in you a fair and honourable opponent; and I feel assured that you do not desire me now to enter in your paper upon a discussion of miracles or of visions. I will therefore add only one more word, which may serve as a rule in estimating the nature of such supernatural facts. We read in the Apocalypse: " I took the book from the hand of the angel, and ate it up, and it was in my mouth sweet as honey, and when I had eaten it my belly was bitter " (Apoc. x. 10). Would it be a sign, I will not say of faith, but common sense, to call this a " physical operation," or to discuss the form, size, and material of this book, or how the physical qualities of sweetness and of bitterness inhered in an object seen in vision, and how it could be eaten? The region of visions is not earthly. They are to be read and understood in the light and by the laws of God's omnipotence.

I would request you to add to your former courtesies by inserting this letter in the *Times* of to-morrow.

I remain, sir, your faithful servant,

HENRY EDWARD,
Archbishop of Westminster.

"EVEN AN ARCHBISHOP."

S. Michael's, Hereford, *Sept.* 28, 1873.

MY DEAR F. GUIRON,

On Wednesday last, as I was coming in the train from Manchester to Worcester, I read for the first time your correspondence with Dr. Nicholson in the *Guardian*.* Until then my knowledge of the whole affair was confined to his first letter, which I read when I gave it to you to answer, and his last, which, as the correspondence was closed, I put, without reading it, into the basket. Of all his intermediate letters I knew nothing, and with your answers my only contact was that I suggested to you certain books and references for your first letter. I remember that I heard you read a paragraph or two of your second; and when I afterwards found that, unknown to me, it was still going on, I told you to waste no more time upon it, and also in what terms to close the correspondence.

Having now read your letters, I think it due to you to say that they are perfectly sound, Catholic, and unanswerable. If you had made any slip in doctrine, I should have taken upon myself the full responsibility—on the just rule, *quod facit per alium facit per se*. I take now the full responsibility of saying that you have not only made no such slip, but have done your work thoroughly well.

It is a just retribution that Dr. Nicholson, who began by accusing me and one of my clergy as either ignorant or unable to defend my words, should after all fall into your hands, and learn to his cost that he had better leave Catholic priests alone.

---

* Dr. Nicholson had accused the Cardinal Archbishop of holding the Sacred Humanity to be Deified or made God, and also of separating the Sacred Humanity from the Divinity and making it a separate and "quasi-God"—two heresies which exclude each other.

His solemn appeals to me all through, and my excommunication as a heretic at last, are very amusing.

I cannot end this letter without saying that I admire in your letters nothing more than the calm, grave, respectful tone with which you bore with an assailant very unlike yourself. It is a sign of the love of truth and of souls. I hope Dr. Nicholson is a young man, for if he be an old one, you, at the outset of your priesthood, have read him a sharp lesson on the manner which befits the treatment of sacred things. He will have learned also that Catholic priests know their theology better than he can teach them, and that it is not safe to accuse even an archbishop. May every blessing be with you and your work.

Believe me always
Yours affectionately in Jesus Christ,
HENRY EDWARD,
Archbishop of Westminster.

"VATICANISM."

To the Editor of MACMILLAN'S MAGAZINE.

October 22, 1874.

SIR,

The author of the article headed *Prussia and the Vatican*, in your October number,* believes that he has detected in me two faults—the one a want of "literary good faith"; the other a deviation from the definitions of the Vatican Council.

The gravity of these charges may be ascertained by the following samples of the author's accuracy:—

I. He quotes, without reference and with evident misunderstanding, a Latin sentence of transparent meaning to all

---

* A series of ignorant articles were appearing in this magazine under the title of " Prussia and the Vatican."

Catholics—*Dominus Petro non solum universam Ecclesiam, sed etiam sæculum reliquit gubernandum.*

He then says: "The Pope is the Vicar of Christ; the temporal sovereign is the Vicar of the Pope."

To this I answer that Catholic theologians hold the three following principles:

1. That the Pope is not the Lord of the whole world.

2. That the Pope is not the Lord even of the whole Christian world.

3. That the Pope has not any purely temporal jurisdiction over temporal princes by Divine right.

Therefore it is untrue to say that "the temporal sovereign is Vicar of the Pope."

II. Again, the author says that "the temporal prince derives his authority from the Pope."

But, as St. Augustine would answer, "*Nemo potest dare quod non habet.*"

Therefore it is again untrue to say that the authority of the temporal prince is derived from the Pope. It is derived from God immediately to civil society, and, *mediante societate,* from God to the temporal prince.

III. The author says further that by the Constitution *Unam Sanctam* all power is in the Pope as all light is in the sun; that the temporal prince has only a borrowed light; and a sword to be used "at the bidding" of the Pope.

I have affirmed, in the essay on *Cæsarism and Ultramontanism,* that the doctrine of the *Unam Sanctam* is as follows:—

1. That there are in the world two powers, both ordained of God, the natural and the supernatural.

2. That of these two the supernatural is the higher.

3. That in its exercise the natural is limited and directed by the law of God.

Such is the doctrine stripped of all imagery of "swords and lights." But it is easier to cavil about words, images, metaphors, and figures, than to face facts and principles. Therefore, if the author means by "bidding" of the Pope that the temporal prince is bound to wield the temporal sword in obedience to the law of God, he is right enough; but if by "bidding" he means the caprice or human passion of the Pope, he shows that my words about common sense were not out of place.

IV. We now come to *The Vatican Council.* I hope the author has not read it; for it does not contain a syllable upon the subject. If he had made this assertion after reading it, I hardly know what to say about literary good faith. But he may mean that the Vatican Council, by defining the Infallibility of the Pope, has raised the *Unam Sanctam* to an *ex-cathedrâ* utterance. It was always so before. The Pope did not begin to be infallible in 1870; nor were Catholics free to deny his infallibility before that date. The denial of his infallibility had indeed never been condemned by a definition, because since the rise of Gallicanism in 1682 no Œcumenical Council had ever been convened. But let us suppose the *Unam Sanctam* to be now binding upon Catholics: it is binding not in the interpretation of the author of *Prussia and the Vatican,* but of the theologians of the Catholic Church; and that interpretation I have given above.

V. "Vaticanism" has indeed shown that between the Christian Church and States without Christianity the *modus vivendi* can only be found by an inflexible refusal to encourage and promote the dechristianizing of education, of literature, of legislation, and of the public and private life of men. If by "cursing modern society" the author means anything more, I must again invoke common sense, and perhaps literary good faith.

VI. But I now come to a matter more difficult of explanation. The author says that in certain articles in the *Contemporary Review* I have kept facts out of sight, and claimed "for Ultramontanism no other rights than those asserted by the Anglican Church and by English Nonconformist sects."

I am afraid the author has read those articles with no more care than he bestowed on reading *The Vatican Council*.

My argument, which was repeated to weariness, was this: "The limitation which has changed Cæsarism into Christian monarchy is law, and that law the law of God, represented, expounded, and applied on earth by an authority of His own creation, and by judicial powers of His own delegation, indedendent of all human legislatures, and superior to all prerogatives of kings." "Now what I have here asserted is Ultramontanism, but it is not Ultramontanism alone—it is Christianity as it has been held by all men, in all ages, by Catholics and by Protestants alike, by Ultramontanes and by Gallicans, by Anglicans and by Presbyterians." (*Cæsarism and Ultramontanism*.)

I see no "keeping back of facts" here. My assertion is this: "Every Christian community claims to be independent of human authority in matter of conscience; and in deciding what is matter of conscience to be superior to all civil powers." In this I say, and say again, Anglicans and all Protestants who retain Christianity—for Erastians can hardly be called Protestants—are agreed. In *this point* Ultramontanes claim no more than Protestants and Anglicans. Where have I ever said that Ultramontanes in other things claim no more?

"All Ultramontanes make these claims." Will the author, therefore, convert the proposition, and say—"All who make these claims are Ultramontanes"?

If he be an Oxford man he is not strong in his Aldrich.

VII. Finally, in a note the author quotes a passage from the *Civiltà Cattolica* of the 18th of March 1871. Now, I can find 20th of March 1871, but no 18th; and in the *Fascicolo*, 20 Marzo, I can find no such passage. I cannot deal with scraps torn from their context without reference, or with an inaccurate reference. But I can clearly see that the meaning here is as transparent to those who wish to see as in the author's anony-

mous Latin quotation. Of one thing, however, I am certain, that its sense is identical with the propositions I have here given from Catholic theologians; and that the author has neither proved a want of literary good faith nor any shade of variation between "Vaticanism" and what is written at Westminster.

I remain, sir, your faithful servant,

HENRY EDWARD,
Archbishop of Westminster.

"OVERCASTING A FRIENDSHIP OF FORTY-FIVE YEARS."

To the Editor of THE NEW YORK HERALD.

Westminster, *November* 10, 1874.

DEAR SIR,

In answer to your question as to my statement about the Vatican Council in the *Times* of yesterday, I reply as follows :—

I asserted that the Vatican Decrees have not changed by a jot or a tittle the obligations or conditions of the civil obedience of Catholics towards the civil powers. The whole of Mr. Gladstone's pamphlet hangs on the contrary assertion, and falls with it.

In proof of my assertion I add :

1. That the infallibility of the Pope was a doctrine of Divine faith before the Vatican Council was held. In the second and third part of a book called *Petri Privilegium* I have given more than sufficient evidence of this assertion.

2. That the Vatican Council simply declared an old truth, and made no new dogma.

3. That the position of Catholics, therefore, in respect to civil allegiance, since the Vatican Council, is precisely what it was before it.

4. That the civil powers of the Christian world have hitherto stood in peaceful relations with an Infallible Church, and that relation has been often recognized by the Church in its Councils. The Vatican Council had therefore no new matter to treat in this point.

5. That the Vatican Council has made no decree whatever on the subject of the civil powers, nor on civil allegiance. This subject was not so much as proposed.

The civil obedience of Catholics rests upon the natural law and the revealed law of God. Society is founded in nature, and subjects are bound in all things lawful to obey their rulers. Society, when Christian, has higher sanctions, and subjects are bound to obey rulers for conscience sake, and because the powers that be are ordained of God. Of all this the Vatican Decrees can have changed nothing, because they have touched nothing.

Mr. Gladstone's whole argument hangs upon an erroneous assertion, into which I can only suppose he has been misled by his misplaced trust in Dr. Döllinger and some of his friends.

On public and private grounds I deeply lament this act of imprudence, and, but for my belief in Mr. Gladstone's sincerity, I should say, this act of injustice. I lament it, as an act out of all harmony and proportion to a great statesman's life, and as the first event that has overcast a friendship of forty-five years. His whole public life has hitherto consolidated the Christian and civil peace of these kingdoms. This act, unless the good providence of God and the good sense of Englishmen avert it, may wreck more than the work of Mr. Gladstone's public career, and at the end of a long life may tarnish a great name.

I remain, dear sir, your faithful servant,

HENRY EDWARD,
Archbishop of Westminster.

"PLAIN ANSWERS IN PLAIN ENGLISH."

To the Editor of MACMILLAN'S MAGAZINE.

La Spezia, *December* 10, 1874.

SIR,

The postscript to an article on *Prussia and the Vatican*, in your December number, needs an answer, and it shall be given. For a writer who affirms that the Head of the Catholic Church claims to be "the Incarnate and Visible Word of God" I have really compassion. Either he sincerely knows no better, and for such exceptional want of knowledge is worthy of all pity, or, knowing better, he is an object of compassion for graver reasons.

I will counsel this gentleman to draw his knowledge from purer and more authentic sources than "Janus," "Quirinus," and the "Old Catholics" of Munich. They will only mislead him. It is profusely evident that he has not yet learnt the first principles of the matter he treats with such confidence in himself, and such contempt of "Vatican Clerics." A writer who believes that the Vicar of Our Lord claims to be "the Incarnate Word" has given to the world the measure of his knowledge, or of his fairness, or of both.

It will be time to discuss the Constitution *Unam Sanctam* with him when he has not only read, but mastered, Hergenröther's *Katholische Kirche und Christlicher Staat*, in which the accusations of the Munich Old Catholics are fully refuted.

The writer disclaims in his article all intention of impugning my "personal good faith." I am glad to hear it, because he did so in his last article; and he has repeated it in the postscript before me. He there clearly implies a charge of duplicity in the use of "the Queen's English." Let me for the last time advise this gentleman to use only the Queen's English, in which he will find none of the nicknames and none of the discourtesies which stain his writings. And also for the last time I will say that an adversary who cannot believe in the honour of those who are opposed to him, not only always strikes wide, but deserves to have his spurs hacked off, and to be led out of the lists of honourable controversy.

What I have publicly affirmed I shall publicly justify, not before your nameless correspondent, but before a tribunal in which I gladly recognize a right to know what I believe and what I teach.

I will now turn to the postscript. In it I find an interrogatory of five questions, followed by these peremptory words—in imitation, it would seem, of a late Prime Minister—not a little comic :—

"I require plain answers in plain English."

I will give them, but not to the interrogator, whose competence I reject. They shall be given plainly and promptly to all into whose hands his interrogative false witness may fall, lest they should be misled by it.

The writer asks :

1. "Did Dr. Manning himself, and the bulk of his clergy, consider themselves before the Vatican Decrees as absolved from their allegiance to the British Crown ?"

Answer.—No.

2. "If Dr. Manning and his clergy did not" so consider themselves absolved, "is it, or is it not, a fact that since the Vatican Decrees they are dogmatically bound, at the peril of their salvation, to consider themselves absolved from that allegiance ?"

Answer.—It is not a fact. Neither I nor they consider ourselves to be absolved from our allegiance ; and the Vatican Decrees have not so much as touched our allegiance.

3. "Is it not certain that the Irish Bishops and the English Vicars Apostolic" "did not consider themselves as absolved from their British allegiance ?"

Answer.—Most certain ; and equally certain that we hold ourselves to be bound equally by that allegiance.

4. "Is there not a risk that a body of officials, not so bound by the ties of allegiance to the Crown of the country in which they are actively employed, and having to obey a code of laws radically different from those of that country, may come into collision with the latter?"

Answer.—Every sentence in this question is either absurd or false. I and my clergy are bound by the ties of allegiance. *Cadit quæstio.* If by "code of laws" be meant civil laws, we have no such code. If by "code of laws" be meant spiritual and religious discipline, there can be no collision, unless Falk laws be introduced into England.

5. "Is Dr. Manning perfectly certain that cases have not already arisen within his own jurisdiction in which clerical persons have been brought into a conflict of jurisdiction," or "have decided (*sic*) since 1870 in favour of the Curial jurisdiction?"

Answer.—I have no knowledge whatsoever of any such cases.

If any such have arisen, they who dealt with them since 1870 otherwise than they would have dealt with them before 1870, have gone astray. The Vatican Council has not so much as touched any such possible question of civil jurisdiction.

Here we return to the sole point in contest.

Before the Council met, a party at Munich prophesied to the world that its Decrees would clash with Civil Allegiances. During the Council they strove in every way to bring down the pressure of the Civil Governments of Europe to hinder the freedom of the Council. The Council steadfastly did its duty, and defined the purely spiritual doctrine of the Authority and the Infallibility of the Head of the Church. It was this they really feared. It is a doctrine they had denied ; and its definition was fatal to their literary authority, and to their personal importance.

From that hour their efforts have been redoubled to bring down the Civil Powers upon the Catholic Church. They have succeeded in setting the German Empire on fire. They are now endeavouring to set fire to the civil and religious peace of our three kingdoms. The whole network of this mischief, the methods and the men, are well known. But it will not succeed. The momentary stir and suspicion, unhappily raised by a great name, will in a little while pass away; and the English people will know not only that the Vatican Decrees have not changed so much as a jot or tittle of our Civil Allegiance, but that Catholics are better evidence as to their own religion than those who are now teaching us the meaning of our Councils, and catechizing us about our loyalty.

I remain, sir, your faithful servant,

HENRY EDWARD,
Archbishop of Westminster.

PAPAL INFALLIBILITY.

To the Editor of the ECHO.

January 12, 1875.

SIR,

I am afraid that I must complain, as you say, once more of your statement in the *Echo* of yesterday evening, purporting to convey what I have written on the subject of the Infallibility of the Pope. What you state is the reverse of what I have written.

Nowhere have I written " that prior to the definition of 1870 *the* voice of the Roman Catholic Church was that of the Episcopate speaking with their Head the Pope."

Convert the proposition and it is true enough. " The Episcopate, speaking with their Head the Pope, is the voice of the

Roman Church." But this was not the only way by which the infallible voice of the Roman Church was heard before 1870. My whole book, *Petri Privilegium*, gives evidence to show " that the Head of the Church, when speaking *ex cathedrâ*, was infallible before 1870." You have, therefore, inverted my whole statement.

In proof of the Infallibility of the Head of the Church speaking *ex cathedrâ*, I have given in the second part of *Petri Privilegium* a whole tradition of witnesses extending over a thousand years.

I have also shown that in the last three hundred years, between the Council of Trent and the Council of the Vatican, the Head of the Church has spoken *ex cathedrâ*, as in the Bull *Unigenitus*, the Bull *Auctorem Fidei*, and the Bull of the Immaculate Conception, all of which have been received as infallible by the whole Church before 1870, on the faith of the Infallibility of the Roman Pontiff, speaking *ex cathedrâ*. I am afraid, therefore, that I must call on you once more to state more correctly what I have written, which is as follows:—

1. That the Episcopate, speaking with its Head, is infallible.
2. That the Head, speaking *ex cathedrâ*, is infallible.

Either way, the voice of the Roman Church is heard.

Your statement, therefore, which excludes the latter proposition, inverts the whole statement and argument of my book, which proves, as I believe, that before 1870, and up to the time of the Apostles, S. Peter and his successors in the Roman See have been, by Divine assistance, preserved from error in faith and morals.

I am sure that you did me this wrong without malice and without guile.

I remain, sir, your faithful servant,
HENRY EDWARD,
Archbishop of Westminster.

"THE GOLDEN TARGET."

To the Editor of THE TIMES.

8 York Place, W., *January* 26 [1873].

SIR,
   Until my return to London yesterday evening I had no opportunity of reading the comments which appeared in your paper of Thursday last on what you supposed me to have said on the preceding Tuesday night at Sheffield. Misled by an account which I do not doubt was given in good faith, but which conveys no report of my words, you have gravely and injuriously misrepresented me. I ask you, therefore, not on personal motives only, but for public reasons, to do me the act of justice of inserting what I did say, with a prominence equal to that of your remarks.

The *Sheffield Daily Telegraph*, which is responsible for the imprudence, if any there be, of reviving on Tuesday last the memory of Lord Denbigh's words, and of making the comments which I considered it then my duty to answer, published on the following day a *verbatim*, and, with few exceptions, a singularly accurate report of what I said.

I will confine myself at present to the two following points :—

You quote as my words that Catholics "cannot identify themselves very closely with a State which admits all creeds and all forms of worship on the same level." Nor can they be " in sympathy with a State which encourages secular education." My words were :—

" How can Catholics, who believe that the faith is one, mingle themselves up in a system which declares that all forms of doctrine are equal ? It is impossible. How can Catholics, who believe that one faith carries with it by necessity unity of worship, regard with sympathy a state of things in which all forms of worship are put upon the same level ? . . . .

How can Catholics, who believe that there should be no education which is not based on the revelation of God, be in sympathy with a state of things in which secular instruction is to be separated from religion?"

You will perceive, Sir, that I spoke of the condition of our present party politics, and in no sense of the British Monarchy.

Your next misrepresentation, as I must call it, is far more serious. You say:—

"If Catholicism is Popery, and Popery, as Dr. Manning avows, is Ultramontanism, and Ultramontanism is allegiance to a foreign Sovereign, there could hardly be a worse recommendation of a Catholic League in English eyes. Unfortunately, these damaging admissions were repeated throughout the Archbishop's speech."

Sir, these admissions are not repeated in my speech. They are not to be found in my speech; they are not to be found even in the garbled account from which you quote. The hypothetical premiss—"if Ultramontanism is allegiance to a foreign Sovereign"—is entirely your own. It is false in law and in fact, as Sir George Bowyer, in his able letter, has already shown. Sir George Bowyer's instincts at once detected that such words as you impute to me could not be mine.

What I did say I here give in the words of the report, which has never been revised by me:—

"I will sum up what I have said in this:—That within the limit and circle of our faith we can compromise nothing—that within that which I will call the gold of the target, we can admit of nothing but the most pure and unalloyed fidelity to the faith of the Church. Outside of that circle, outside of what I may call the gold of the target, in all things which relate either to the social welfare or to the political well-being, to the peace and stability of the country and of the empire, there are no men on the face of England who are more loyal, there are no men who are more patriotic than Catholics. In our allegiance to the faith we admit of no compromise, but there are no men in England who are more patriotic in all things which are outside the question of faith than the Catholics of the British Empire. Nay, I will go further, and will say there are no men who are more ready to labour for the well-being of the country, for its political peace, for its political progress, for its social order, for its industry, its commerce, and for its education, than are the Catholics of this country. Now, I can conceive no subject in which Catholics are unpatriotic. I can conceive no subject in which Catholics can be in collision with the laws of the British Empire, so long as the laws of the British Empire are not in collision with the laws of God."

The error into which you have been led is this :—You represent me as saying that there is in the civil allegiance of Catholics a circle which is reserved for some other, and, you say, foreign authority. I affirmed that this circle surrounds our faith, outside of which our loyalty is as pure and true as that of other men ; and I will add, what Sir George Bowyer has well said, that it is our faith that dictates our loyalty.

I forbear, at present, from all further comments on your article, save only this,—I am at a loss to see how our public peace can be promoted by holding me up as an example of disloyalty. As an Englishman, I am as sensitive on this point as you can be ; but you will, I think, see that as your words cannot affect me only as a private person, they may have an effect which neither you nor I should desire.

I have no doubt, Sir, that you will make the act of reparation which is due to me by inserting this letter in your paper of to-morrow.

I am, Sir, your faithful servant,
HENRY EDWARD,
Archbishop of Westminster.

"THE LIVING CONSCIOUSNESS OF THE CHURCH."

To The Congregation of the Oblates of S. Charles.*

Ash Wednesday 1875.

Reverend and dear Fathers,

Nearly ten years ago I dedicated to you a very slender book on "The Temporal Mission of the Holy Ghost." And now once more I have another, which traces at least the outline of the same subject.

The former book was on the special office of the Holy Ghost in the One Visible Church, which is the organ of His divine voice. The present volume deals with the universal office of the Holy Ghost in the souls of men. The former or special office dates from the Incarnation and the Day of Pentecost; the latter or universal office dates from the Creation, and at this hour still pervades by its operations the whole race of mankind. It is true to say with S. Irenaeus, *Ubi Ecclesia ibi Spiritus—* "Where the Church is there is the Spirit;" but it would not be true to say, Where the Church is not, neither is the Spirit there. The operations of the Holy Ghost have always pervaded the whole race of men from the beginning, and they are now in full activity even among those who are without the Church; for God will have all men to be saved, and to come to the knowledge of the truth.

I have therefore, in this present volume, spoken of the universal office of which every living man has shared, and does share at this hour; and I have tried to draw the outline of our individual sanctification. Nobody can be more fully aware how slender and insufficient are both these books. They are only put out as provocations, in the hope of rousing you to fill up the outline.

* The dedication of "The Internal Working of the Holy Ghost." (Burns & Oates.) 1875.

It is my hope that some of you may be stirred up to edit, in one volume, the treatises of S. Didymus, S. Basil, and S. Ambrose, on the Holy Ghost; and also certain portions of S. Bonaventure, S. Thomas the Carthusian, and S. Bernardine of Sienna, on the Graces and Seven Gifts of the Holy Ghost, and on the Beatitudes which spring from them. These united would make a precious store for students and for preachers.

My belief is that these topics have a special fitness in the nineteenth century. They are the direct antidote both of the heretical spirit which is abroad, and of the unspiritual and worldly mind of so many Christians. The presence of the Holy Ghost in the Church is the source of its infallibility; the presence of the Holy Ghost in the soul is the source of its sanctification. These two operations of the same spirit are in perfect harmony. The test of the spiritual man is his conformity to the mind of the Church. *Sentire cum Ecclesia*, in dogma, discipline, traditions, devotions, customs, opinions, sympathies, is the countersign that the work in our hearts is not from the diabolical spirit, nor from the human, but from the Divine.

S. Ambrose, S. Francis, S. Philip, S. Teresa, had an ardent devotion to the Holy Ghost. S. Teresa, in her Life, tells us that one day, after Mass, on the vigil of Pentecost, in a very retired place where she often used to pray, she was reading a work on the Feast of Pentecost by a Carthusian. I have always thought and hoped that it may have been the work of Dionysius, from whom I have quoted in these pages. His spiritual treatises are of singular beauty and depth, uniting the subtilty and accuracy of a scholastic with the spiritual light and sweetness of a mystical theologian.

It would seem that the development of error has constrained the Church in these times to treat especially of the third and last clause of the Apostles' Creed : " I believe in the Holy Ghost, the Holy Catholic Church, the Communion of Saints."

The definitions of the Immaculate Conception of the Mother of God, of the Infallibility of the Vicar of Christ, bring out into distinct relief the twofold office of the Holy Ghost, of which one part is His perpetual assistance in the Church, the other His sanctification of the soul, of which the Immaculate Conception is the first-fruits and perfect exemplar.

The living consciousness which the Catholic Church has, that it is the dwelling-place of the Spirit of Truth and the organ of His Voice, seems to be growing more and more vividly upon its pastors and people, as the nations are falling away: *Hi sunt, qui segregant semetipsos animales, Spiritum non habentes.* This prophecy of the Apostle is visibly fulfilling before our eyes; while the unity, outward and inward, the unanimity and supernatural expansion of the Catholic Church by its own imperishable life and intrinsic force, bear witness of a Presence, a Mind, a Will, and a Power which is not of man, but of God. We seem to see and to touch the evidence of the promise, "I will ask the Father, and He shall give you another Paraclete, that He may abide with you for ever. It is expedient for you that I go; for if I go not, the Paraclete will not come to you; but if I go, I will send Him to you, the Spirit of Truth, Whom the world cannot receive, because it seeth Him not, nor knoweth Him; but you shall know Him, because He shall abide with you, and shall be in you."

My purpose, however, is not to enter upon this large field in a preface, but only to commend to you, as the matter of your special study and the burden of your constant preaching, "the ministration of the Spirit," under which we are. S. Ambrose says: "*Si appellare dominum Jesum sine Spiritu non possumus, utique sine Spiritu prædicare non possumus.*" I can desire for you, therefore, no better gift than that you may all be *pleni Spiritu Sancto et Sapientia. Et vos, unctionem quam accepistis ab Eo, maneat in vobis. Et non necesse habetis ut aliquis doceat vos; sed sicut unctio ejus docet voce de omnibus, et verum est, et non est mendacium. Et sicut docuit manete in Eo.*

Believe me, reverend and dear Fathers,
   Yours very affectionately in Jesus Christ,
     HENRY EDWARD,
      Archbishop of Westminster.

"AS MY TIME GROWS SHORT."

To the ENGLISH STUDENTS OF THE UNIVERSITY OF LOUVAIN.

    Archbishop's House, Westminster, S.W.,
      June 18, 1875.

You will, I hope, believe that my long delay in thanking you for your address of congratulations * has arisen from no want of appreciation on my part.

I have been steadily replying, as my heavy duties allow me the time, to the many similar expressions of confidence and goodwill. But I have not as yet been able to reply to all.

I now thank you from my heart for your filial words, and I pray God that you may bring home into England the high intellectual culture of a Catholic University to aid in raising the intellectual maturity of our Catholic people.

It is a happiness to me to know that as my time grows short there are young men fresh and green in the vigour of youth and faith to take up the work we must soon lay down. There is a future in England for all who are the disciples of the See of Peter. *Doctores fidelium Ecclesiae discipuli.*

May God perfect this spirit in you, and keep you always in His holy fear.

    HENRY EDWARD,
     Cardinal Archbishop of Westminster.

* On the occasion of the Archbishop's elevation to the Cardinalate.

"THE ONLY HONOUR."

To CANON O'SULLIVAN, V.G.*

Archbishop's House, Westminster,
July 10, 1875.

I thank you, and through you, as President, the Association of the Venerable College of St. Thomas de Urbe, for the words of congratulation and confidence addressed to me at your last meeting.

You will, I believe, all of you accept my assurance that, though not an alumnus, I am a true, and loyal, and old friend of the English College at Rome. I have from time to time lived within its walls so long as to amount to years. Every part of it is as familiar to me as if it had been my home. Its memories and its traditions are sacred to all Catholics; and for the last years I have had the official duty of watching over its safety.

Be sure therefore that though I have not my predecessor's right to be a patron of your association, I have the will to be in every way united with you.

I thank you all for what you say to and of myself. You will give me your prayers that I may never be wanting in the duties which the Holy Father has been pleased to lay upon me. The times are not times of peace, and the only honour is to be in the front in time of need.

May God multiply, and prosper, and consolidate the Association of St. Thomas de Urbe!

Believe me, &c.,

HENRY E.,
Cardinal Archbishop of Westminster.

* Canon O'Sullivan had presented on behalf of the Association of the Venerable College of St. Thomas de Urbe an address of congratulation.

DANIEL O'CONNELL.

To the LORD MAYOR OF DUBLIN.*

London, *July* 28, 1875.

MY DEAR LORD MAYOR,

I return you my very sincere thanks for your lordship's kindness in inviting me to take part in the centenary of Daniel O'Connell's birth, and I beg you to convey to all who are acting with you my regret that it will be impossible for me to be present. Had it been in my power to be with you, I should have expressed in no uncertain words the gratitude of Catholics in England to the man whose prudence, firmness, eloquence, and devotion won for the Catholic Church in these realms its liberation from penal laws.

To him is due, under God, more than to any other, that Ireland is an united people, growing year by year in power and prosperity. I am old enough to remember O'Connell's first entrance into the Legislature, and how in him and by him the Catholics of these kingdoms became an integral part of the public opinion and of the Legislature of the Empire. But I believe it will be for posterity to appreciate fully the work which he accomplished from that day. The Catholic Church in our country has become a part of our national life, and our fellow-countrymen have seen its worship and heard its voice, and are beginning to regard it with respect and goodwill as one of the most powerful and beneficent influences of our social order. Daily and intimate contact with Catholics has swept away old controversies. And in bringing about this pacific change Daniel O'Connell stands as the foremost man.

I rejoice to hear the noble and pathetic answer of the Bishops of Germany to your timely invitation. I hope the good Pro-

---

* Peter Paul M'Swiney was Lord Mayor at the time of the O'Connell Centenary Celebration.

vidence of God will raise up in Germany from among its Catholic laity a man who shall lead them to the restoration of liberty of conscience and of the Church.

Believe me, my dear Lord Mayor, your faithful servant,

HENRY EDWARD, CARDINAL MANNING.
Archbishop of Westminster.

"IN THE DAYS OF ANXIETY."
To the BISHOP OF PORT LOUIS.*

Archbishop's House, *July* 30, 1875.

MY DEAR LORD,

I hope that neither your Lordship nor your good clergy will believe for a moment that I have been insensible to your great kindness in conveying to me your sympathy and goodwill in what the Holy Father has been pleased to lay upon me.

In truth, since I came from Rome, the press of correspondence coming upon my ordinary work, already beyond my time, has caused me to fall into a great arrear. Let me now heartily thank you and your excellent priests. They will, I hope, pray for me that in the days of anxiety, which are upon us, and may hereafter be still darker, I may have light to see, and strength to do, what the Holy See requires of its servants.

In return I will not fail to ask that the spirit of unity and charity, and zeal for souls, may be abundantly poured out upon the Church and Diocese of Port Louis.

Believe me, my dear Lord, yours affectionately in Jesus Christ,

HENRY E.,
Cardinal Archbishop of Westminster.

* Who had sent on behalf of himself and his clergy a letter of congratulation.

"THE APPEAL TO HISTORY."

To the Editor of THE DAILY TELEGRAPH.

Archbishop's House, *October* 15, 1875.

SIR,

Lord Redesdale's courteous letter * in your paper of to-day is one more example in proof of the statement that my critics suppress my argument instead of answering it.

"If the voice of the Church be, by Divine assistance, infallible," then to appeal from it, to whatsoever tribunal, is to reject a Divine authority. This is clearly both treason and heresy.

What Lord Redesdale has to show is "that the voice of the Church is not, by Divine assistance, infallible." This he has

---

* Lord Redesdale had written as follows :—" Cardinal Manning gives the following as the correct extract from 'The Temporal Mission of the Holy Ghost' : 'The appeal to antiquity is both a treason and a heresy. It is a treason because it rejects the Divine voice of the Church at this hour, and a heresy because it denies that voice to be Divine.' And defends it by stating his argument to be as follows : 'The appeal from the living voice of the Church to any tribunal whatsoever, human history included, is an act of private judgment and a treason, because that living voice is supreme; and to appeal from that supreme voice is also a heresy, because that voice, by Divine assistance, is infallible.' He adds : 'I have seen much misrepresentation of my argument, but I have never seen an answer. Unless the premisses can be refuted no answer can be made.' I accept the challenge. The Church of Rome refuses the cup to the laity who come to her to receive the Sacrament of Christ's Body and Blood. I desire the Cardinal to give, if he can, prompt, separate, and explicit answers to the three following questions :—First. Is it treason and heresy to say that history informs us that when Christ instituted that Holy Sacrament He ordained that His blood was to be given and received through the wine as well as His body through the bread, and that all ought now to receive the Sacrament in the manner He ordained ? Second. Is it treason and heresy to say that antiquity informs us that in the time of the Apostles and long afterwards all who received that Sacrament partook of the wine as well as the bread, and that we ought all now to do as they did? Third. When and how was the Church of Rome Divinely instructed to order what is directly contrary to what Christ Himself ordered when on earth by express words?" The other topics and twistings put forth by Lord Redesdale in subsequent letters will be sufficiently explained by the terms of his Eminence's replies.

not done, nor attempted to do. I, therefore, answer his questions as follows :—

1. Our Lord ordained that the Holy Sacrament should be consecrated and received by His Apostles in both kinds, but He did not ordain that it should be received by all Christians in both kinds.

2. Communion in both kinds was in use for centuries, and is in use in some places at this day, but not as a necessary obligation by Divine commandment. We therefore are not all bound to Communion in both kinds.

3. The Church was Divinely instructed in all things relating to doctrine and discipline by the advent of the Spirit of Truth on the day of Pentecost, who, according to the promise of Our Lord, abides for ever in the Church.

Lord Redesdale will find my proof of this truth in the book he has quoted. Until he has refuted this premiss, which my critics have always suppressed, he is only begging the question once more. I therefore affirm that, to say, as he implies, that Communion in both kinds is necessary to all is both treason and heresy; not because it is an assertion intrinsically erroneous in itself, but because it is an assertion made in contradiction to an authority which is Divine. This point Lord Redesdale has avoided; but it is the point of my argument which he was bound to refute.

I remain, Sir, your faithful servant,

HENRY EDWARD,
Cardinal Archbishop.

"A DIVINE AUTHORITY."

To the Editor of THE DAILY TELEGRAPH.

Archbishop's House, Westminster,
October 22 [1875].

SIR,
Your readers must, I fear, be weary of the subject, but I must not be so far wanting in courtesy to Lord Redesdale as

not to reply to his letter. I must once more call his attention to the fact that he has both begged the question and changed it. The question between us is simply this : " Is it heresy to appeal *from* a Divine authority ? " You, Sir, were clear-sighted enough to see that to appeal *from* a Divine judge to any human tribunal whatsoever must be unlawful. What Lord Redesdale has to show is, " that the authority of the Church is not Divine." Instead of proving this he has assumed it ; and he then affirms that it has erred. Let him say whether the authority of the Church be Divine or not. If it be Divine no appeal can lie from it.

If he say that it is only human I must ask him to read the book he has referred to, " The Temporal Mission of the Holy Ghost." If, after reading it, Lord Redesdale shall still say either that the Spirit of Truth does not guide the Church, or that the Church, guided by the Spirit of Truth, can err in faith, I shall then have an answer to the question which he has hitherto begged.

On the question of the lawfulness and sufficiency of Communion " in one kind " I shall then be ready to give a full statement. But at this time it is irrelevant.

It is not relevant to say the authority of the Church is not Divine because it has ordained Communion in one kind. It can only be proved not to be Divine by the evidence proper to the question, " What is the authority with which the Divine Founder of the Church invested it ? "

As I cannot ask you, Sir, to reprint a book in your columns I must refer your readers to the work already named, in which I have given, as I believe, full and sufficient proof of the Faith.

I remain, Sir, your faithful servant,

HENRY EDWARD,
Cardinal Archbishop.

"HOLY SCRIPTURE IS SCRIPTURE ONLY IN ITS RIGHT SENSE."

To the Editor of THE DAILY TELEGRAPH.

Archbishop's House, *October* 27 [1875].

SIR,

Lord Redesdale is a little too confident of victory. He has not yet put off his harness. His letter of to-day contains some matters which, I believe, on reflection he will think, as I do, to be irrelevant. I will therefore still confine myself to our argument. Neither Lord Redesdale, nor any man, can show that the authority of the Roman Church is not Divine because it "refuses the Cup to the laity"—I am using his words—until he shall have first shown that the obligation to receive Communion in both kinds is, by Divine commandment, imposed upon all Christians.

This he has not done.

It is not enough to quote the words of Holy Scripture until he has proved that he uses them in their true sense. Holy Scripture is Scripture only in its right sense ; as a man's will is his will only so long as it is rightly interpreted. I deny Lord Redesdale's interpretation, and he has not proved it to be the true one. But he has once again begged the question. "Is this interpretation the true sense of Holy Scripture?" Till he has proved this he has done nothing.

In my first letter I pointed out that the words of institution of the Holy Sacrament were addressed, not to all Christians, but to the Apostles. They, like the command to baptize and to absolve, are a commandment to the Apostles. They commanded the Apostles to consecrate and to receive the most Holy Sacrament in both kinds. They do not command all Christians to communicate in both kinds, any more than they command all Christians to consecrate the Lord's Supper. Will Lord Redesdale affirm this latter proposition ? If Lord Redesdale says that the commandment to consecrate the Holy Sacrament is given to all Christians I need make no farther reply. I may leave the controversy in the hands of most of the Bishops and most of the clergy of the Anglican Church. They will answer him. He must choose one of two things: the commandment is either universal or not universal. If he say it is universal as to Communion, he must show how it is not also universal as to Consecration. If he say it is not universal as to Consecration, he must show that of which he has not shown the shadow of a proof—namely, how is it an universal command as to Communion.

I reject Lord Redesdale's interpretation of Scripture: and in quoting this text he is simply begging the question: "Is this the true sense of Scripture?"

Finally, Lord Redesdale says: "I hold the authority of Christ to be Divine, and that it is heresy to appeal from it. So far I agree with the Cardinal."

I have nowhere said anything so useless. I said, "the authority of the Church is Divine." And that proposition Lord Redesdale cannot disprove except by refuting its proper evidence. He does not advance his argument a single point by reiterating the quotations from Scripture about Communion. The Sacramentarians would quote against Lord Redesdale the same words that he quotes against me, and would tell him that they are "the authority of Christ" to prove that the Bread and Wine are merely figures.

As I said in my last letter, Lord Redesdale has to show one of two things—"either that the Church is not guided by the Spirit of Truth, or that the Church guided by the Spirit of Truth can err in faith."

I have affirmed its authority to be Divine because it is guided by the Spirit of Truth; and that, for that same reason, to appeal from its authority is heresy. I have also referred Lord Redesdale to the proper evidence of this assertion. Let him refute it. All else is, I do not think it becoming to say "shirking," but beating the air.

I remain, sir, your obedient servant,

HENRY EDWARD,
Cardinal Archbishop.

"COMMUNION IN ONE KIND."

To the Editor of THE DAILY TELEGRAPH.

Archishop's House, *October* 30 [1875].

SIR,

Lord Redesdale asks me to give the reason why the Catholic Church has ordered Communion in one kind only to be received by all, whether priests or lay people, excepting only the celebrating priest. This I am most willing to do. But I must forewarn him that, if he shall say that the Catholic Church is wrong in its interpretation of Holy Scripture—which would be assuming, without saying it, that he is right—he must bear with me if I still repeat, first, that he is begging the question, "Which of the two interpreters cannot err?" and secondly, that, instead of showing that the evidence given, in the book so often named, to prove "that the Catholic Church is guided always by the Spirit of Truth," is insufficient, he has proposed to me to discuss "Communion in one kind." I must therefore say again that he has changed the question. But I am very willing for the present to follow him.

The main reason why the Catholic Church ordered Communion in one kind is given in the Catechism of the Council of Trent. It was to eradicate the heresy of those who denied that the presence of Christ is whole and perfect under either kind. They affirmed that the body alone, without the blood (*corpus exsangue*), is present under the form of bread, and the blood alone under the form of wine. This was a gross, earthly and carnal conception, like that of the people of Capharnaum. The Church, in the Councils of Constance and of Trent, therefore condemned it, and declared that in either kind was contained the whole and undivided presence of Christ. The practice of Communion in one kind was enjoined to test the faith of those who received it.

For the same reason, in the time of the Manichean heresy, Pope Gelasius and Pope Leo I. ordered that none should be admitted to Communion who would not communicate in both kinds. The Manicheans refused the chalice because they taught that wine came from an evil principle. Communion in both kinds detected them.

The doctrine of the Church on this subject is as follows:—
"There is no Divine commandment nor any intrinsic necessity that all men should receive Communion in both kinds."

1. First, there is no Divine commandment. The argument in my last letter is still unanswered. The words of our Lord are a command to the Apostles and to their successors only. The consecration in both kinds, and the consuming of both, are necessary to the sacrifice of Christ, continued and represented in the Sacrament of His body and blood. The priest who consecrates receives both—not as if both were necessary to Communion, but because the consuming of both is necessary to the sacrifice.

2. Secondly, there is no intrinsic necessity to receive both. Communion in either is full and perfect. The words of our Lord in St. John prove this, and disprove the interpretation of Lord Redesdale. Our Lord says, in three places: "I am the living bread. . . . . If any man shall eat of this bread he shall live for ever" (chap. vi. 51, 52). Again: "The bread which I will give is my flesh for the life of the world" (v. 52); and again, "He that eateth this bread shall live for ever" (v. 59). Lastly: "As the living Father hath sent Me, and I live by the

Father, so he that eateth Me, the same shall also live by Me" (v. 58); that is, "as I am consubstantial with the Father as God, they that eat Me shall be consubstantial with Me as man." "He that eateth Me, in that one act partakes both of the body and of the blood; and he that eateth this bread eateth Me." It is a gross, earthly, and carnal error to suppose that Communion is divided, or that each of the two kinds contains severally that which is not present in the other.

Lord Redesdale strangely imagines that I make a concession in saying that Communion in both kinds was long in practice, and is still in practice in some places at this day. Throughout the whole of those ages Communion was given also in one kind to the sick, to those who were in prison, to households in time of persecution, and in other circumstances of necessity. Even the Greek Church at this day gives Communion to the sick in one kind only.

Now I have made this answer simply out of courtesy. Lord Redesdale says that in denying his interpretation of Holy Scripture I beg the question as much as he does. Let us try the comparison. I deny that our Lord's words bind all Christians to receive in both kinds. The whole Catholic Church at least denies it with me, and, I might add, the Greek Church also.

Lord Redesdale denies that our Lord's words are a command to consecrate the Lord's Supper. I shall be curious to see who share with him in this denial. Not the Lutherans, who hold consubstantiation. Not the genuine Calvinists, for they hold a real presence. Not the Anglicans, from Bishop Andrews to Bishop Wilson, for they profusely believed in the act of consecration. Not, I think—though I have my fears—the pious and reverent Evangelical clergy, for they somehow believe the Communion Service. Lord Redesdale will find himself, I think, in a scant and ill-sorted company.

Be so good as to observe that I say nothing of the promise

that the Spirit of Truth shall abide with the Church for ever. This was our thesis at first, but for Lord Redesdale's sake we have left it.

Lastly, I must not omit to add that we are not on equal terms; Lord Redesdale has the advantage of me. He knows precisely what I hold, for the Council of Trent tells him. I do not at all know what he holds, for the Church of England does not tell me. Negatively I can gather that he does not hold transubstantiation, for the Thirty-nine Articles expressly reject it. But positively I can have no knowledge. I know what Bishop Andrews held, for he said, "Take away your transubstantiation, and we have no quarrel with your Sacrifice;" and I think I know what the Sacramentarian Churchmen hold, but between these two distant regions I do not know where Lord Redesdale may be. His former letters give little sign, his last gives less. The most definite passage seems to be that in which he denies that in the Lord's Supper there is any Consecration, but only a universal command to receive. To receive what?

But, as I said, I leave this to the bishops and clergy of his own Church.

I remain, sir, your faithful servant,

HENRY EDWARD,

Cardinal Archbishop.

THE TEACHING CHURCH.

To the Editor of THE DAILY TELEGRAPH.

Archbishop's House, S.W., *November* 3 [1875].

SIR,

I see with sincere regret that I have unconsciously given Lord Redèsdale pain. Some of his words I indeed thought a little too free, and it seemed to me not amiss that he should be sensible of it. But I have too much respect for him to forget what is due to him and to myself; and I hope I may add that his letters may be misunderstood without wilful misunderstanding. Henceforth I will treat of the subject he has proposed without reference to myself.

It is self-evident that if the Catholic Church can be convicted of violating a Divine commandment it cannot, in that at least, be guided by the Spirit of Truth ; and if it can be shown that Communion in both kinds is enjoined upon all the faithful by a Divine commandment, the Catholic Church, in decreeing Communion in one kind, would have violated a Divine commandment.

It rests upon those who make this charge to prove that such a Divine commandment exists. Not a shadow of such a proof has as yet been made.

I. The words of institution by Our Divine Saviour contain no such Divine commandment. He consecrated bread and wine. He commanded the Apostles to do the same in commemoration of Him. He commanded them both to eat and to drink that which He consecrated. When Our Lord commanded His Apostles to baptize all nations, He gave a Divine commission to be executed and regulated in its exercise by the Apostles and their successors. The obligation to receive baptism is distinct from the commission to baptize. In like manner, when Our Lord breathed upon His Apostles He gave them power, and a commandment to remit or to retain the sins of men. The obligation to receive such absolution is wholly distinct from the commission to absolve, and is not here expressed.

In these three commandments or commissions these is not a word as to the mode of receiving Communion, or baptism, or absolution. The Council of Trent defines that, in the command to consecrate, Our Divine Lord communicated to the Apostles a share in His own priesthood. There is not, in the quotations which have hitherto been introduced into this correspondence from the New Testament, a word to prove a universal obligation laid upon all the faithful to communicate in both kinds. They abundantly, indeed, prove that the practice of Communion in both kinds existed. But this nobody denies. What is denied, and what must be proved, is that this practice was by Divine commandment. It was at that day the practice to baptize by immersion. There are those who still say that baptism by immersion is a Divine commandment. By what authority then was baptism by affusion introduced throughout the Church ? By the same authority which introduced Communion in one kind.

II. We will now go to see whether the practice of Communion in both kinds imposes any obligation whatsoever upon all the faithful. Again, it is for those who affirm it to make good their assertion. Nevertheless, I will give evidence to show that, from the earliest traceable records, it is proved that the practice of Communion in both kinds, and the practice of Communion in one kind, existed simultaneously and ran on side by side.

Dr. Döllinger, whose weight will probably be greater with some for the same reasons which with us make it to be less, in his "History of the Church" says: "The Blessed Eucharist was ordinarily administered to the faithful in the ancient Church under both forms of bread and wine; but there never was a doubt that the substance of the Sacrament was contained entire under either form; or that he who received under either form received a perfect Sacrament." . . . . "Communion under one form was . . . . frequent in the ancient Church; perhaps more frequent than Communion under both forms. For domestic Communion, in which the faithful partook only of the consecrated bread, which they had taken with them to their houses, was, particularly in times of persecution, of more ordinary occurrence than Communion in the Church." Of this there is evidence in Tertullian as early as about the year A.D. 200. Dr. Döllinger adds that the anchorets in the wilderness communicated only in one kind. So also the sick. He gives the example of Serapion and of St. Ambrose, who when dying received in one kind only at the hands of the Bishop Honoratus. This was in A.D. 397. He adds the practice of the Greek Church, in which, during Lent, Communion was given five days in the week in one kind only. ("History of the Church," vol. ii. 323-325; translation by Dr. Cox.)

I may refer to another book equally accessible, the "Hierurgia" of Dr. Rock. He says: "So far .... is the Greek Church from considering Communion under the two species as essential to the integrity of the Sacrament that during the whole of Lent, except on Saturdays and Sundays and the Feast of the Annunciation, the Mass, as it is called, of the Presanctified—*i.e.*, in which there is no Consecration—is alone permitted. . . . . Consequently the Greek priest who offers up the Mass, as well as those amongst the laity . . . . take the Holy Communion under one kind only—that of bread." "Moreover, in the Greek Church the Viaticum, or Eucharist, given to the dying, is administered on all occasions, and at every season of the year, under the sole form of bread alone. The same is the practice of the Maronites and other Oriental Christians." He further asserts that this practice came from the time of the Apostles, and quotes evidence from the second and third centuries. ("Hierurgia," vol. i. pp. 273-282.)

To this I may add two cases of Communion in one kind only which are mentioned by Venerable Bede in his "History of the Anglo-Saxon Church" in the 14th and 24th chapters of the Fourth Book—that is, in the century after the restoration of Christianity in England. Is it possible that such facts could be mentioned without reproof if there were a Divine command to receive in both kinds? Objectors have to disprove these facts, public and authoritative, sanctioned by the earliest ages, by the greatest saints, and by the practice of the whole Church, East and West, before they can venture to affirm, on their private interpretation of the Scripture, that there is a Divine command to receive in both kinds.

Communion in both kinds and Communion in one kind were alike in practice and in the same ages and places throughout the Church, and as we have seen, the ages nearest to the Apostles, which is an historical demonstration that neither any Divine command nor any intrinsic necessity for Communion in both kinds was ever believed to exist. The error is modern, and sprang from two roots—a carnal doctrine about the Real Presence, and private interpretation of Holy Scripture.

III. I will now repeat the answer given in my first letter as to the authority by which Communion in one kind was ordered. It was by the Divine authority of the Church, guided by the Spirit of Truth, the sole witness, teacher, and judge as to what commandments are Divine, and how far they extend.

In the question before us, the Church from the beginning—and, to preclude objection, I will add, before the division of East and West—taught that no Divine commandment existed binding all the faithful to Communion in both kinds ; and it sanctioned, as the facts above cited prove, the practice of Communion in one kind only. There was in this no claim to an authority superior to a Divine commandment. No such commandment in this case existed. The Church had, and it exercised, a Divine authority to declare what commandments were Divine, and what was the extent of their obligation. I found this assertion upon the passage to which I am referred, St. Matthew xxviii. 19, 20, by which the following truths are proved :—

1. That Our Lord constituted the Apostles to be the teachers of all nations.

2. That He commanded the Apostles to baptize those who believed in the unity of the faith.

3. That He committed to the Apostles the custody of His commandments, and made them to be the teachers and the interpreters of the same.

4. That He promised His own abiding presence with the Apostles, and with those who bear the apostolic office, until the end of the world.

This, in my judgment, will be sufficient to prove that the Church has a Divine authority to declare what are the commandments committed to it, and that an appeal from its Divine voice in such declarations is resistance to a supreme authority, and therefore treason, and a rejection of a Divine authority, and therefore heresy. But these are no new crimes newly invented; they are the moral obliquities of unbelief, as old as the Divine authority against which they offend.

But we have not yet stated the full proof of this Divine authority of the Church. After Our Divine Lord has given this commission to His Apostles, and constituted them the witnesses and teachers of His commandments—and, I must add, the sole fountain of His supreme jurisdiction in the world—He commanded them not to depart from Jerusalem until they should be endued with power from on high (Acts i. 4, 5). He had said to them before His passion, "It is expedient for you that I go, for if I go not the Paraclete will not come to you; but if I go I will send Him to you" (St. John xvi. 7). And again: "I will ask the Father, and He will give to you another Paraclete, that He may abide with you for ever" (xiv. 16). From these words of Our Divine Lord it may be affirmed:

1. That when he ascended to the Father the Holy Ghost personally came as another Paraclete in His stead.

2. That the mission of the Son into the world ended at His ascension; but that the personal presence of the Holy Ghost in His stead abides for ever.

3. That the Paraclete came, according to his promise, upon

the Apostles and upon the Church which they founded throughout the world.

4. That the Paraclete, or the Spirit of Truth, abides still in that Church of all nations which alone is spread throughout the world.

For these reasons I affirm the authority of that Church to be Divine, and all appeals *from* its authority in matters of faith to be what I will not repeat. Finally, once more to preclude objections, I will add that this one Church of all nations was from the beginning in communion with its centre at Rome; that it is so at this moment; that the Church is therefore both Catholic and Roman; that "the Catholic Church" and "the Roman Church" are coincident titles and realities; and that its authority as a teacher rests upon the promise of its Divine Head, and upon the abiding presence of the Spirit of Truth.

I remain, sir, your faithful servant,
HENRY EDWARD,
Cardinal Archbishop.

"LORD REDESDALE OR S. AMBROSE."

To the Editor of THE DAILY TELEGRAPH.

Archbishop's House, *Nov.* 6 [1875].

SIR,

Lord Redesdale says that he has closed this correspondence on his part. I hold it to be a sound rule to be the last to begin a contention and the last to leave off. I did not begin this correspondence. And neither on the 24th of October, nor in my last letter, did I give any sign of desiring to close it. My object is, not to gain a victory over Lord Redesdale, but to vindicate the Divine authority of the Catholic Church from an imputation of having erred.

Let us, however, now sum up. Lord Redesdale's whole argument consists in this. He says the Church has erred. To prove this he quotes a text, and he interprets that text of Scripture in a sense at variance with the interpretation held by the whole Church, Greek and Latin, East and West ; and confirmed, as I have shown, by the traceable practice of the Church running up to the second century, and sanctioned by the judgment and the example of the greatest names of the Christian world.

The immemorial practice of Communion in one kind is not to be disposed of by talking of persecution, or of "exceptional cases." Its antiquity and widespread use prove beyond contention two things : firstly, that the words of Our Lord in instituting the Holy Sacrament conveyed no Divine commandment imposing upon all the faithful to receive in both kinds ; and secondly, that, to the full integrity of Communion, it was held to be absolutely indifferent whether Communion was received in both kinds or in one alone. A "mutilated Sacrament"—as Lord Redesdale called it—would be a sacrilege, both in the giver and receiver. Were the early Christians in the East and West habitually sacrilegious ? Did St. Ambrose on his deathbed receive a "mutilated" Sacrament? Did he make a sacrilegious Communion before appearing in the presence of his Lord ? Would he have listened to Lord Redesdale if he had stood by his dying bed to inculcate the doctrine contained in his letters ? We must believe either Lord Redesdale or St. Ambrose ; and I am content to leave this issue to the judgment of common sense, to which Lord Redesdale has appealed.

I have said from the beginning that the whole of this correspondence is a begging of the question.

Not one hair's-breadth beyond this has Lord Redesdale advanced his argument.

Lord Redesdale can claim for his interpretation of the words of Scripture no higher certainty and no higher authority than his own, and the authority of those, be they few or many, who proceed, as he does, on the same principle of private opinion. The certainty and authority upon which I rely for the interpretation that I have given, is the authority of the Catholic Church, which, as I proved in the close of my last letter by the full and plain words of Our Lord Himself, is preserved always from error in faith by the perpetual presence and assistance of the Spirit of Truth. This was my original thesis ; and against this not one relevant argument has hitherto been directed.

I remain, sir, your faithful servant,

HENRY EDWARD,
Cardinal Archbishop.

"SIN EVEN IN AN ANGEL."

To the Editor of THE DAILY TELEGRAPH.

December 14 [1875].

SIR,

Lord Redesdale has attempted to show that the authority of the Catholic Church is not divine, because it has erred ; and he has endeavoured to show that it has erred, because it has ordained Communion to be received in one kind. To prove this, Lord Redesdale has affirmed that the words of Our Lord in instituting the Holy Sacrament impose a command upon all Christians to receive it in both kinds. In answer I have shown :—

1. That this interpretation of Our Lord's words is contrary to the interpretation of all ages down to the outbreak of modern controversies.

2. That it is contrary to the immemorial practice of the

Church, which has, from the earliest traceable antiquity, maintained the practice of giving Communion in private in one kind only. Communion in both kinds was given in public, and Communion in one kind was given in private, from the second till the twelfth century. Communion in one kind, then, gradually prevailed till the Council of Constance, for wise and evident reasons, ordained that Communion in one kind should thenceforth be the rule both in public and in private. What is sufficient in private is sufficient in public ; no Divine command to the contrary existing. If this is " evasion," what is directness ?

Lastly, I have given proof from the words of Our Lord in Holy Scripture :

1. That the Spirit of Truth, by His perpetual presence and perpetual assistance, preserves the Church from error in faith.

2. That the Voice of the Church is therefore Divine, because it is the Voice of the Spirit of Truth. " He that heareth you, heareth me."

This has never been met by a shadow of relevant argument.

It would, indeed, be a grave thing to deny the perpetual presence and assistance of the Spirit of Truth in the Church. But this Divine Truth must be denied before it can be shown that the Catholic Church has erred. If the Spirit of Truth be with it for ever, the conclusion is inevitable.

To appeal from the Divine Voice to any other tribunal is both treason and heresy. And these high spiritual crimes are not "newly invented" by the Catholic Church. They are moral obliquities, as I have long ago shown, as old as the Divine Authority against which they offend. To appeal from this Gospel, which the Apostle preached, is that " other Gospel" which St. Paul says would be sin even in an angel.

I remain, sir, your faithful servant,

HENRY EDWARD,
Cardinal Archbishop.

TEMPERANCE.

Addressed to FATHER LOCKHART.

Archbishop's House, *Passion Sunday*, 1877.

To the Members of the League of the Cross and to all my flock who have come together in honour of the Feast of St. Patrick, by promoting in themselves and others one of the virtues that St. Patrick loved best.

Until to-day I had been earnestly hoping to take my place among you to-morrow night, but I now see that it will be out of my power. I am kept to the house by an ailment, which, though in no way serious, has given me fourteen days of constant pain. You know that I would be with you if I could, and I know that you would not wish me to come at the risk of being made worse.

I am the more sorry that I cannot be with you, because for the first time a number of good Catholic laymen, who have never been with us before, have promised to come and give their help to the work of the League of the Cross.

You do not need many words from me. I trust that to-morrow night many will make up their minds to give up the use of all intoxicating drink. I call especially upon those who in time past have fallen under its power, or are in danger *now*, to give it up, as they hope for the salvation of their souls; and I call also on those who have never fallen, and are in no danger at this time, to give up intoxicating drink as an example to others who are in danger; for their encouragement and help, and to make reparation and expiation for the sins that are being committed by drunkenness everywhere and every day. I call especially upon fathers, for the sake of their wives and children, and upon mothers for the sake of their homes; and I earnestly pray you to bring up your children from their earliest years in complete abstinence from all intoxicating drink: if they had never tasted it they would never have been tempted. If you give it them they will learn to love it, and when once they have learned to love it they may soon be beyond your control and their own.

May the blessing of God rest upon you, and give you strength to stand steadfast and to persevere in total abstinence.

HENRY EDWARD,
Cardinal Archbishop.

"THE REVIVAL OF THE ROMAN QUESTION."

To the Editor of THE DAILY NEWS.

March 27, 1877.

SIR,

Under the above title, your correspondent, writing from Rome, as it appears in your number of to-day, makes the following statement:

"Lord Derby actually promised to the Catholic party in England that he would give diplomatic support to the foreign Powers who would espouse the cause of the Holy See. The announcement of this promise (says my Vatican informant) came through Cardinal Manning."

So far as my knowledge extends, the above paragraph, from first to last and in every particular, is absolutely without foundation.

I make no comment upon the highly mischievous character of this fabrication.

I remain, sir, yours obediently,

HENRY EDWARD,
Cardinal Archbishop.

DR. WARD AND THE *DUBLIN REVIEW*.

To the late W. G. WARD.*

Archbishop's House, Westminster,
November 7, 1879.

MY DEAR DR. WARD,

Our Holy Father, Leo XIII., by a letter from the Cardinal Secretary of State, commands me to inform you that his Holiness has been pleased to confer upon you the *commenda* of the Order of St. Gregory, and at the same time to make

---

* William George Ward, of Northwood Park, Isle of Wight, was born in London in 1812. His father, Mr. William Ward, was for many years M.P. for the City ; and he was a director of the Bank of England at the same time as the father of Cardinal Manning. Dr. Ward was educated at Winchester and at Christ Church, Oxford ; and was elected in 1834 Fellow of Balliol on the same day as Archbishop Tait. In 1841 he published his pamphlets in defence of Tract 90, and was in consequence deprived, by Dr. Jenkyns, Master of Balliol, of his tutorship. In 1844 he published " The Ideal of a Christian Church," for which he was deprived of his degrees in full Convocation at Oxford. In March 1845 he married the youngest daughter of the Rev. John Wingfield, Prebendary of Worcester and Canon of York. In September, Father Brownbill, S.J., received Mr. and Mrs. Ward into the Church. In 1853 Dr. Ward was appointed, by Cardinal Wiseman, Professor of Dogmatic Theology at Old Hall College, Ward having a few years previously come into possession, by the death of his uncle, of the Ward property in the Isle of Wight. In reward for his services at Old Hall, Pius IX. made him a Doctor of Philosophy. In 1863, at the request of Cardinal Wiseman and Provost Manning, he undertook the editorship of the *Dublin Review*, and conducted in it his polemics against J. S. Mill, which have since been republished under the title of " The Philosophy of Theism " (C. Kegan Paul, Trench & Co.). He was one of the founders of the Metaphysical Society, and was its chairman at a time when Gladstone, Ruskin, Martineau, Huxley, Tyndall, Tennyson, and the Duke of Argyll were among its members. He retired from the editorship of the *Dublin* in 1878, and spent the remaining years of his life in the republication of some of his anonymous works. In 1880 Leo XIII. created him Commendatore of the Order of St. Gregory the Great, in recognition of his work in the *Dublin Review*. He died in July, 1882, at Hampstead. A Memoir of Dr. Ward, containing some account of the later scenes of the Oxford Movement, and a considerable correspondence with Cardinal Newman, Pusey, J. S. Mill, and others, is now being prepared by his son, Mr. Wilfrid Ward.

known the motives which have prompted the Holy Father to bestow on you this distinguished mark of confidence.

His Holiness is fully aware of the fidelity and labour with which in the last seventeen or eighteen years you have devoted yourself and your means to the conduct of the *Dublin Review*, and to your other writings for the vindication of the doctrinal authority of the Holy See and of its civil rights. The Holy Father knows also how forward and able a defender you have been of Christian and Catholic philosophy against the manifold aberrations of modern metaphysics, and against the theories which, in rejecting metaphysics, altogether deny the evidence of reason and of sense, together with the freedom of the will, thereby undermining all morality.

It was with this information before him that the Holy Father desired the Cardinal Secretary to write as follows :—That "this distinction is conferred on you in testimony of the high esteem in which his Holiness holds the services rendered by you to the Church and to science, especially in philosophy, by the publication of your works ; and of the great satisfaction with which the Holy Father sees a Catholic layman employing the lights and talents which Divine Providence has bestowed upon him for the defence of the rights of the Roman Pontiff which have been violated, and for the diffusion of doctrines against which the self-called philosophers of our times direct their attacks."

Believe me, my dear Dr. Ward,
Your affectionate servant in Christ,
HENRY EDWARD,
Cardinal Archbishop.

"THE UNITY WHICH BINDS THE CATHOLICS OF IRELAND AND OF ENGLAND TOGETHER."

To the late A. M. SULLIVAN, M.P.

July, 1881.

MY DEAR MR. SULLIVAN,

I have received the address of the Catholic members for Ireland to our Holy Father Leo XIII., on the late abominable outrages in Rome, together with the private letter signed by yourself and Mr. Bellingham.*

It gives me a very sensible pleasure to be the channel of communication between the members for Ireland and our Holy Father, and I am sure that his Holiness will see in it an evidence of the unity which binds the Catholics of Ireland and of England together. This will be all the more manifest by the fact that your address, which is now being translated into Italian, will be presented to the Holy Father by the Cardinal-Secretary, together with a letter written by me, in the name of the whole Episcopate of England.

So far I have spoken of our public relations; but I cannot fail to thank you for the concluding paragraph of your letter. It gives me consolation to know that the little I have been able to say or to do for Ireland is not unknown to you and to the Irish people, and that you think it deserving of such expressions as you have used.

---

* Reference is here made to the riots attending the re-interment of the body of the late Pontiff, Pius IX. In asking the Cardinal Archbishop to present to Leo XIII. their protest, Mr. Sullivan and Mr. Henry Bellingham, acting as secretaries for the Irish Catholic members, concluded their letter to his Eminence with these words :—" We gladly avail ourselves of this opportunity of renewing for ourselves and for our country the expressions of that profound reverence and affectionate regard which it has so often been to us a pleasure and a duty to testify towards your Eminence, whose words of wise counsel and tender sympathy are always gratefully esteemed by the Irish people."

I request you to convey this reply to those whom you represent.

> Believe me, my dear Mr. Sullivan,
> Yours very faithfully,
> HENRY E.,
> Cardinal Archbishop of Westminster.

"IF YOUR READERS ONLY LAUGH AT ME."

To the Editor of MERRY ENGLAND.*

> Archbishop's House, Westminster, S.W.
> *December* 16, 1884.

MY DEAR MR. MEYNELL,

I am ashamed of myself; but the enclosed may go; and if your readers only laugh at me, it will make merry England merrier.

> Yours affectionately,
> HENRY EDWARD,
> Cardinal Archbishop.

---

* The hurried note given in facsimile was written by his Eminence when sending one of the Essays his pen has contributed to MERRY ENGLAND. Its reproduction here gives an opportunity for publicly acknowledging a kindness which never fails—a kindness which does not permit on the lips of the busiest man of the century the plea, "I have not time," when a Catholic interest is in question—a kindness which never pauses to ask what posterity will say or contemporaries think of an article thrown off at odd moments on a topic imposed by editorial tyranny, yet backed by a great name, since he is told that by publishing it a Catholic Magazine will greatly gain. Such self-forgetfulness is read about in edifying books, and is counselled in many pulpits. But the practice of it, in all editorial experience, is strictly limited to one solitary class of the community—the Cardinal Archbishops.

ARCHBISHOP'S HOUSE,
WESTMINSTER,
S.W.

Dec. 16. 1904

My dear Mr Meynell,

I am ashamed of myself but this inclosed may go & if your readers only laugh at me it will make Merry England merrier.

Yours &c
H. E. C. A.

FEDERATED EMIGRATION.

To ARNOLD WHITE.

Archbishop's House, Westminster, S.W.
April 10, 1885.

DEAR MR. WHITE,

Most unfortunately the meeting on the subject of emigration at the Westminster Palace Hotel, to which you have invited me, falls on a day in which it is impossible for me to attend; but the great interest that I have taken for so many years in the work of emigration induces me to express what I think on the proposed meeting.

If I understand it rightly, it is to call together all those who are at this time engaged in promoting emigration, without regard to the manifold diversities, religious, political, or otherwise, which may at the present divide us. I should have been glad to come above all for this reason, believing as I do, and as I have endeavoured for many years in practice to show, that, while we must all inflexibly adhere to the dictates of conscience in matters above the things of this world, we are bound, nevertheless, as members of the same commonwealth, heartily to unite together in all works of public utility, and especially of benevolence and beneficence, for the people.

In saying this I do not mean that the existing emigration societies should merge themselves in one. I believe that coalitions are generally weak and paralyze the amount of energy which before was possessed by independent bodies, and I have greater faith in the harvest that springs from many ploughs going at once in the same field, so long as they do not cross each other's furrow. But it is evident that close mutual intelligence and mutual co-operation ought to exist among those who are engaged in such a common duty for the good of the people as their safe and provided emigration to our Colonies. All parts of the Empire ought to be regarded as only an extension of the Mother Country, where our people may always feel themselves at home.

I will add, lest I should seem to forget it, that in this common co-operation, where we are all working on the same paths and to the same end, I do not in the least forget the separate religious care and provision which we should all alike make for those who belong to our several responsibilities. I believe that this united action in that in which we agree, and distinct private provision for that in which we may differ, can by mutual respect and mutual confidence be most efficiently maintained.

Believe me, always yours faithfully,

HENRY E.,
Cardinal Archbishop.

"OFFICIALLY BOUND TO NEUTRALITY."

To C. J. MUNICH.*

Archbishop's House, *Nov.* 11, 1885.

DEAR SIR,

I am sorry to have been so slow in returning the enclosed, and replying to your question. In truth I have been laid up with a severe cold.

It would seem to me that voters must vote, after all, according to their own convictions. It is not unreasonable or in any way wrong to try to convince a voter of what we believe to be right or better. But beyond this we have no right or duty.

* A Catholic elector of the Strand district, who, during the contest of 1886, appealed to the Archbishop for a pronouncement on the relative claims of Mr. W. H. Smith, M.P., and his Liberal opponent, the latter having also declared in favour of placing the schools where definite Religion is taught on an equality with those of the Board.

I always hold myself to be officially bound to neutrality, and leave my clergy and flock perfectly free.

Believe me, dear sir, yours faithfully,

HENRY E.,
Cardinal Archbishop.

"JOY IN BELIEVING."

To the ARCHBISHOP OF TORONTO.

Archbishop's House, Westminster, S.W.,
February 24, 1886.

MY DEAR LORD ARCHBISHOP,

I thank your Grace, and through you many others, who have sent to me the forged letter* which has been published as mine. On last Saturday, as soon as it reached me, I telegraphed to your good Dean to expose this imposture. What good the forger thought to gain I don't know, but I may turn his handiwork to good account.

It gives me the opportunity to say that from the hour I saw the full light of the Catholic faith, no shade of doubt has ever passed over my reason or my conscience. I could as soon believe that a part is equal to the whole as that Protestantism in any shape, from Lutheranism to Anglicanism, is the revelation of the day of Pentecost. As to my friends, the priests here and in many lands, they have been to me my help and consolation; and as to the conversion of others, my last five-and-thirty years have been spent in receiving them into the Church.

I am glad to take this occasion which the forger has made

* This forged letter was printed in the Canadian newspapers, and purported to be addressed by his Eminence to Lord Robert Montagu.

for me to bear once more my thankful witness to the Catholic Church. The worst I wish him is, that his eyes may be opened to see the truth, and the unworthiness of his own act.

Believe me, my dear Lord Archbishop,
Your affectionate servant in Christ,
HENRY E.,
Cardinal Archbishop of Westminster.

THE PRIMROSE LEAGUE.

To A. TEIXEIRA DE MATTOS.

Archbishop's House, Westminster, S.W.,
March 18, 1886.

DEAR SIR,
There is no prohibition in this diocese as to the Primrose League.

In the first draft of its rules the members engaged to support Religion as by law established. This no Catholic could do. The draft was revised, and there is now nothing that a Catholic may not promise. The engagement is to maintain religion or Christianity and freedom of conscience against atheism and atheistic or anti-Christian politics.

I remain, dear sir, yours faithfully,
HENRY E.,
Card. Archbishop.

1885.

Landmarks of a Lifetime.

HENRY EDWARD MANNING,
CARDINAL ARCHBISHOP OF WESTMINSTER.

Born July 15, 1808, at Totteridge, Herts; the son of Mr. William Manning, sometime M.P. for Evesham, for Lymington, and for Penryhn, and Governor of the Bank of England.

Educated at a private school in Totteridge, and afterwards at Harrow and at Balliol College, Oxford, where he took his B.A. degree in 1830, and a First Class in Classics.

Entered the Colonial Office in 1831, in preparation for a political career, which had always had a fascination for him, and for which he fitted himself by a close study of Constitutional Law and of Political History.

Under a growing sense of duty towards Religion, he resigned his post at the Colonial Office in 1832, and returned to Oxford, where he was elected Fellow of Merton.

Took Orders in the Anglican Church at Christmas 1832; and in 1833 accepted the Rectories of Lavington and Graffham in Sussex.

In 1838 took a leader's part in the Educational movement by which Diocesan Boards were established all over England; also in opposition to the secularization of Church of England property by the creation of Ecclesiastical Commissioners.

Appointed Archdeacon of Chichester in 1840, and Select Preacher to the University of Oxford in 1842.

On Passion Sunday 1851 was received into the Catholic Church.

Ordained Priest in the summer of 1851, and passed some four years in study at the Academia Ecclesiastica, a Pontifical College situated in the Whitehall of Rome, and established to finish the training of men who had elsewhere taken their degrees, and who were destined for high diplomatic and ecclesiastical duties as Nuncios and otherwise—a very nursery of Cardinals, whose portraits covered the corridor walls. Thither the future English Prince of the Church went by the advice of Pius IX., and it was at this time that the acquaintance with his Holiness, which the young priest had begun while he was still an Anglican Archdeacon, ripened into an intimacy which years made only more tender and more profound.*

Took degree of Doctor of Divinity in 1854.

Visited the Oblates of St. Charles Borromeo at Milan in 1856, and then proceeded to Rome, where a Rule, founded on theirs, was drawn up, and received the benediction of Pius IX.

Founded the Congregation of the Oblates of St. Charles at Bayswater 1857, taking possession of the house on the night of Whit-Sunday.

Appointed Provost of Westminster in 1857, and Protonotary Apostolic in 1860.

Consecrated Archbishop of Westminster in succession to Cardinal Wiseman in June 1865.

Attended the Vatican Council in 1869 and 1870.

Removed in 1873 from 8 York Place, W., the lease of which he had inherited from Cardinal Wiseman, to Archbishop's House, Westminster, the freehold of which he has secured to the Archdiocese.

Summoned to Rome by Pope Pius IX. in March 1875, to be raised to the rank of Cardinal, taking his title from the Church of St. Gregory on the Cœlian Hill.

Served on Royal Commission on the Housing of the Poor in 1885, and on the Royal Commission on the Education Acts in 1886.

---

* His Eminence has paid twenty-one visits to Rome, two of which were previous to his conversion. The first of these was in May 1848, when the young Pontiff received him at the Quirinal, and spoke much of England, mentioning with admiration Mrs. Fry and the Quakers, and saying, "When men do good works, God gives grace. My prayers are offered every day for England." It may be added that the Pontiff when on his deathbed recurred to that first meeting, and reminded his friend that it was just forty years since they had met, and in what different relations!

www.ingramcontent.com/pod-product-compliance
Lightning Source LLC
Chambersburg PA
CBHW020301090426
42735CB00009B/1172